Critical acclaim for *Adventure Guide to the Everglades & Florida Keys*:

"The Everglades will always be mysterious, but finding them? —it doesn't have to be! This book makes it easy to discover the whole region, even the secret places like Corkscrew Swamp."

Ed Carlson
National Audubon Society

"...vastly informative, absolutely user friendly, and chock full of the kind of interesting information that makes me want to put the book under my arm, pack my gear and leave immediately to investigate those places so well described. ...from trails to historic sites to underwater adventure, it is all there..."

Dr. Susan P. Cropper, DVM,
Society of Aquatic Veterinarians

"...a great book—practical and easy to use. The perfect traveler's guide to these two beautiful and ecologically sensitive areas."

Ted Wesemann
Director, Wilderness Southeast

D0880148

AUTHOR'S NOTE

Encounters with wildlife highlight many visitor tours to south Florida. Whether you are watching an osprey nesting atop a light pole, an alligator traversing an Everglades trail, or a school of grunts along a coral wall you will gain a memorable glimpse into a magical world.

Visitor interpretations of these "magical glimpses" are often more interesting than what's actually going on. Our favorite is from a diver who, upon sighting mating turtles, rushed to the nearest ranger station to report: "Please help! There is a turtle in trouble and another is trying to hold it up!"

Understanding exactly what the animals are doing is tough. Overall, when in doubt, it is safest (for them and for you) to give them a wide berth.

To find out a bit more we went to marine-animal specialist Dee Scarr, author of *Touch the Sea, The Gentle Sea*, and numerous animal-behavior articles. Following are her tips:

"We've grown up watching "nature" on television, where hours of animal behaviors are edited down for us to a few minutes of intensely exciting action. This cheats us by not showing more of the animals' subtle behaviors. Before your trip to the Everglades or Florida Keys, read as much as you can about the resident animals—marine life, native birds, for example, and alligators. Then, while at your observation post, consider what the animal is doing while bearing in mind that all animals must, among other things, breathe, feed themselves, avoid predators and reproduce.

Is that alligator resting, or is it keeping a sharp eye on some nearby, but not-quite-close-enough prey? The inhabitants of a coral reef aren't aimlessly wandering around; some are munching on algal growth, others are plucking microscopic planktonic life from the water, still others, like the alligator, are waiting for a prey animal to get just a little closer.

Picking a single critter and watching it for ten or twenty minutes at a time will give you a much better sense of what its life is like than simply scanning all the animals and being disappointed because they're not "doing anything". Remember, even if an animal isn't active, it's usually doing something—it's up to you to figure out what that something is! "

Adventure Guide
To The
EVERGLADES
&
FLORIDA KEYS

Joyce Huber
Jon Huber

MPC
HUNTER
PUBLISHING INC

Hunter Publishing, Inc.
300 Raritan Center Parkway
Edison NJ 08818 (908) 225-1900

ISBN 1-55650-494-2

© 1994 Hunter Publishing, Inc.

All rights reserved. No part of this publication may be
reproduced, stored in a retrieval system, or transmitted in any
form, or by any means, electronic, mechanical, photocopying,
recording or otherwise, without the written permission
of the publisher.

Printed in the U.S.A.

Published in the UK by:
Moorland Publishing Co. Ltd.
Moor Farm Rd, Airfield Estate
Ashbourne DE6 1HD
England

ISBN (UK) 0-86190-460-0

Photo Credits

Larry Mulvehill: Seven-Mile Bridge; Key West from the Air.
Joyce Huber: Kayak, Key Largo. Bill Dayner: Seaplanes at Fort Jefferson.
Stuart Newman & Associates: Key Deer; Diver on the Duane.
All others by Jon Huber.

Maps by Joyce Huber.

CONTENTS

ACKNOWLEDGEMENTS

The enthusiasm and assistance of the following people made an invaluable contribution to this guide. Special thanks to our publisher, Michael Hunter; Carol and Larry Mulvehill; Jean Gomez, Stuart Newman Associates; Pat Tolle, Gene Cox, Everglades National Park; Warren Zeiller, Everglades Visitor Association; Sandra Higgs, Monroe County Tourist Development Council; Dee Scarr; Coco Higgins; Dr. Susan Cropper; Brenda Fine; Bob Epstein, Wildwater Productions; Bill Anderson, Old Island Restoration Foundation; Ed Carlson, National Audubon Society; Jean, Douglas and Oliver Prew; Dale and Pat Conway; Randy Pegram, Captain Todd Firm, John Pennekamp State Park; Captain Bill Wickers; Claudia Sammartino; Camille Mancuso; Ted Wesemann, Wilderness Southeast; Nadia and Jim Spencer; Pam and Dave Heddiwick; Barbara Swab; Louise and Dave Perlstein; Mike and Yuri, F-Stop Graphics; Ed Davidson, Biscayne Aqua-Center; and Barbara Swab.

NOTE: Extreme caution should be exercised while participating in ocean, river or other sports. Know your own skill and endurance limits. Training and fitness or certification requirements should be checked well in advance of your trip. Expedition leaders, divemasters and park rangers can be of help. Weather and sea reports should be obtained immediately prior to entering the water. The authors, contributors, and publishers of this guide assume no liability for its use.

SECTION I

PLANNING
YOUR TRIP

A unique range of recreational choices combined with a sub-tropical climate attract more than two million visitors to Everglades National Park and the Florida Keys each year. Whatever the outdoor adventurer has in mind, there seems to be a perfect place for it in this part of the world. Activities exist for every age, fitness, and experience level.

Whether you choose to settle in the Everglades or the Keys you are near enough to explore the mysteries and surprises of the other.

When to Go

Visit Everglades National Park from December through March, the dry season. The rest of the year brings torrential downpours and mosquitos which cloud the air and cluster in gobs on your skin the moment you enter the park. We found bugs a problem as late as mid-November, particularly in Flamingo.

The Florida Keys high season has traditionally been from December through May though many divers and snorkelers prefer the calm and warmer waters of summer. In winter skies are predictably sunny and air temperatures range from 75 to 85° F.

Fall brings chance of a hurricane, but offers lower hotel rates and often beautiful weather.

Salt-water fishing is big all year. Comfort-wise, angling the "back-country" is best in winter, but good fly-fishing in the bays is more dependent on a full or new moon than the season. This desired, high-tide period occurs twice a month and is published in the tide tables.

Key West attractions are best seen during winter months. While summer trade winds offer a bit of relief to the other islands, Key West's maze of city buildings blocks the flow. The island is uncomfortably hot during July and August.

Adventure Tours

Money-saving tour packages for air and hotel can be arranged by any travel agent. Several outfitters offer all-inclusive canoe-camping expeditions through the Everglades, Biscayne and Florida Keys (see Canoe chapter). Dive shops throughout the U.S. offer group trips that include transportation, diving and accommodations. Snorkelers often may join for a lower rate. Every major resort in the Florida Keys offers a dive-accommodation package as do many of the Keys dive shops (see diving and accommodation chapters for listings). Day and half-day sailing, fishing, and snorkeling tours are offered throughout the area. See specialty chapters for listings.

Handicap Facilities

Most of the larger resorts have full handicap facilities. The state and national parks have wheelchair-accessible trails, tour boats, accommodations, restaurants. The following dive operators offer certification and dives for the handicapped based on "degree of handicap and skill of the diver": Captain Billy's Key West Dive, MM 4.5. U.S. 1, Stock Island, Key West (1-800-87-DIVER or 305-294-7177); Key West Pro Dive, 1605 N. Roosevelt Blvd., Key West (305-296-3823); Reef Raiders Dive Shop, 109 Duval St., Key

West (305-294- 3635); Lost Reef Adventures, Land's End Village, 261 Margaret St. (1-800-633-6833 or 305-296-9737); Looe Key Dive Center, Ramrod Key (1-800-942-5397); Sea Center Dive Shop, Big Pine Key (305-872-2319); Strike Zone Charters, Big Pine Key (1-800-654-9560); John Pennekamp State Park, Key Largo (305-451-1202); Biscayne Aqua-Center, Convoy Point, Homestead (305-247-2400) has wheelchair access for their tour, snorkel & dive boats, though no special certifications. Theatre of the Sea, Islamorada has wheelchair ramps into the attraction area and the swim-with-the-dolphin pools.

For updated information contact the individual resorts and facilities.

GETTING THERE

All major national and international airlines fly into Miami Airport. There are scheduled flights from Miami to Marathon and Key West. No regularly scheduled public transportation exists to Everglades National Park.

Driving from the North, take Florida Turnpike to Exit 4 —Homestead Key West. From Tampa take 1-75 south to Naples, then east to Miami and the Turnpike Extension or 41 South, then east to the Turnpike Extension, then south to U.S. 1.

To The Everglades

Flamingo. From Miami Airport, take LeJeune Road south to 836 West, then the Turnpike Extension south to U.S. 1. Turn right off U.S. 1 in Homestead onto State Highway 9336. An 11-mile ride will bring you to the park entrance and the Main Visitor's Center. From there it is a 38-mile trip along the Main Park Road to Flamingo.

Tamiami Trail. From Miami, it is 45 miles to Shark Valley and 95 miles to the Gulf Coast Ranger Station and Everglades City. Driving from Miami Airport, take LeJeune Road south to 836 West, then Florida's Turnpike south to Route 41, the Tamiami

Trail. It is a 45-mile ride to Shark Valley and the Miccosukee Indian Reservation. To reach the Gulf Coast Ranger Station, Everglades City and the Ten-Thousand-Island region, continue an additional 40 miles along Route 41 West to Route 29 South. Then go three more miles to the ranger station. Total distance from Miami to the Gulf Coast area is 95 miles.

To The Florida Keys

To reach the Keys from Miami International Airport, take LeJeune Road south to 836 West. Then take the Turnpike Extension to U.S. 1, which runs the length of the Florida Keys to Key West.

MILE MARKERS

Mile Markers are used throughout this guide to reference locations in the Florida Keys. They appear on the right shoulder of the road (U.S. 1) as small green signs with white numbers and are posted each mile beginning with number 126, just south of Florida City. Mile markers end with the zero marker at the corner of Fleming and Whitehead streets in Key West. Awareness of these markers is useful as Keys' residents use them continually. When asking for directions in the Keys, your answer will likely be at, just before or just beyond a milemarker number.

By Bicycle

Florida's turnpike does not allow bicycles and U.S. 1 in parts is devoid of a shoulder and dangerous for road riding. Cyclists are advised to transport their bikes by car from the airport to the Everglades or the Keys. Greyhound will transport your bike to points along U.S. 1 if the bicycle is boxed (see Cycling chapter). Rentals are widely available.

Public Transportation and Rentals

At Miami Airport: Avis, Budget, Hertz, National and Value. If possible, book rental cars in advance of your trip. In season you may be forced to rent more car than you planned.

PHONE NUMBERS FOR RENTAL CARS:

Alamo 1-800-327-9633

Avis 1-800-331-1212

Budget 1-800-527-0700

Dollar 1-800-421-6868

Hertz 1-800-654-3131

National 1-800-227-7368

Thrifty 1-800-367-2277

PHONE NUMBERS FOR CABS:

Miami

Checker Cab 888-8888

Yellow Cab 444-4444

Diamond Cab 545-7575

Seven Star Limo 238-2400

Key Largo - Tavernier

Sailboat John's Taxi, Inc. 852-7999

Island Taxi 664-8181

Marathon

Island Taxi 743-0077

Paradise Taxi 743-3141

Out-Island Taxi 743-8500

Big Pine Key

Island Taxi 872-4404

Key West

Checker 294-2594

Better Cab 294-4444

Yellow Cab 294-2227

Everglades City Area

Naples Taxi   775-0505

PHONE NUMBERS FOR TRAINS

Amtrak   1-800-872-7245

Metrorail (Miami) 638-6700

BUSSES

Greyhound buses leave three times daily (7 a.m., noon and 6 p.m.) from the airport-vicinity bus station at 4111 N.W. 27th Street, Miami. One-way fare to Key West is $36 (subject to change). Travel time to Key West is 4 1/2 hrs. Phone: 305-876-7123.

The Homestead terminal is at 5 N.E. 3rd Road, Homestead FL 33030. Phone: 305-247-2040.

By Boat

Boaters can reach the area by the inland waterway or outside via the Gulf or Atlantic. The Intracoastal Waterway is limited to shallow draft vessels (5 ft or less). Deep draft boats enroute to Key West follow Hawks Channel which passes between the outer reefs and the Florida Keys. The Coast Guard monitors VHF 16.

NOAA CHARTS

11451 - For small craft traveling from Miami to Marathon and Florida Bay

11465 - Intracoastal Waterway from Miami to Elliott Key

11463 - Intracoastal Waterway from Elliott Key to Islamorada

11462 - Fowey Rocks to Alligator Reef

11452 - Alligator Reef to Sombrero Key

11550 - Fowey Rocks to American Shoal

11449 - Islamorada to Bahia Honda

11448 - Intracoastal Waterway - Big Spanish Channel to Johnson Key

11445 - Intracoastal Waterway from Bahia Honda to Key West

11441 - Key West Harbor and approaches
11447 - Key West Harbor

Gulf Coast

11429 - Naples to Pavilion Key
11431 - Pavilion Key to Florida Bay area

Bareboating and Crewed Yacht Vacations

Fully-equipped live-aboard motor yachts and sailboats with or without crews can be chartered from the following organizations:

ATLANTIC COAST

Captain Danny Valls
Cruzan Yacht Charters
P.O. Box 53
Coconut Grove FL 33133
1-800-628-0785

Cruzan offers a large selection of O'Day, Watkins, Hunter and Sunward sailing yachts from 30' to 50'. Sample rate for an all-inclusive week for party of six aboard a 50' crewed Sunward would start at $5200.

Treasure Harbor Marine, Inc
200 Treasure Harbor Drive
Islamorada FL 33036
1-800-FLA-BOAT
305-852-2458

Treasure Harbor Marine offers day sailboats and live-aboards. Prices range from $110 per day for a 19' day sail to $375 for a 44' uncrewed live-aboard. By the week from $395 to $1595.

Florida Keys Motoryachts
P.O. Box 456
Key Largo FL 33037
1-800-443-4667
305-451-2221

Motoryachts, houseboats, and sailboats—crewed or bareboat.

Witts End
Marina Del Mar Docks
MM 100
P.O. Box 625
Key Largo FL 33037
305-451-3354

Crewed charters aboard Witts End, a 51-ft ketch.

ON THE GULF COAST

Fort Myers Yacht Charters
14341 Port Comfort Road
Fort Myers FL 33908
813-466-1800

Captained, bareboat and lessons.

Private Plane

There are some restrictions for private aircraft flying into the Keys. For example, as of December, 1990 light planes must have 12-inch registration numbers and a mode C transponder. A flight plan is required for some areas. Before entering the area contact Aircraft Owner's and Pilot's Association for a current briefing. Phone: 301-695-2140. Or write AOPA Flight Operations Department, 421 Aviation Way, Frederick, MD 21701. For water landings additional information may be available from the Seaplane Pilot's Association at 301-695-2083. The Miami sectional covers the area.

WHAT TO BRING

Clothing

Clothing should be lightweight and casual. Shorts and tee shirts cover most fashion needs though one change of dressy attire may prove useful. In the Everglades long pants and long-sleeved shirts offer some protection from bug bites. Bring sunglasses and a hat that will shade your face.

Gear

See individual adventure chapters for details. If you are joining a special interest tour group avoid mix-ups by labeling all you bring. Colored plastic tape and permanent marker are waterproof.

Most canoe-camping outfitters provide everything needed for a wilderness expedition except transportation from the airport and clothes. Tents, canoes, meals, sleeping bags, air mattresses are included in most packages. Check with individual operators (see Canoe chapter).

Dive packages often include use of tanks and weights. Bring or plan to rent everything else. Snorkeling equipment is provided by the boat-tour and seaplane operators, but bringing your own insures a comfortable fit (see Dive and Snorkeling chapters).

Charter and party boats provide fishing gear. Just bring a cap with a wide brim. The marina stores are well-stocked with tackle and other gear. Polarizing sunglasses such as Cabela's, Corning Serengeti Strata or Rayban are best for spotting fish in the mangrove flats.

Hikers wishing to explore off-the-beaten-track trails should wear submersible shoes. Bring the type with a non-slip sole that won't tear on sharp rocks. We find the new aqua socks made by Nike or Omega or strap-on kayaking sandals perfect for sloshing around mangrove islands, beach combing and walking on coral rubble.

Sundries

Some form of mosquito repellent is necessary, especially in Summer. The Main Visitors Center at Everglades National Park sells a popular brand. Florida Keys shops are well-stocked year round.

Off-season (March 15 - Nov. 15), travelers to the Everglades should pack some of everything needed before entering the park. Restaurants outside the park will pack you a lunch.

Credit Cards

With the exception of some small motels, major national and international credit cards are widely accepted throughout the Florida Keys. Money machines are found in the populated areas of the Keys. Personal checks are accepted in some stores with ID—a driver's license and a major credit card. You need a major credit card to rent a car. Restaurants and stores in Everglades City do not accept credit cards.

INSURANCE

Standard Blue Cross and Blue Shield policies do cover medical costs while traveling. Lost luggage insurance is available at the ticket counter of many airlines. If you have a homeowner's policy, you may already be covered. Some credit cards also cover losses while on vacation. Membership in the American Automobile Association covers unexpected road emergencies for auto travelers.

Inexpensive insurance for rental-car mishaps is available from the rental agencies and well worth the price.

Visitors from Great Britain may obtain traveler's coverage from Europ Assistance, 252 High St., Croydon, Surrey CRO 1NF. Phone: 01680-1234.

Scuba divers can get health insurance to cover accidents or emergencies which are a direct result of diving for a low annual fee from Diver's Alert Network (DAN). A stay in a recompression chamber can amount to thousands of dollars and is often not covered by standard medical insurance. For information stop in your local diveshop or write to DAN, P.O. Box 3823, Duke University Medical Center, Durham NC 27710. Phone: 919-684-2948.

HELPFUL PHONE NUMBERS

Emergency (Police, Ambulance, Fire) : 911

Everglades General Information: 305-247-6211

Shark Valley: 305-221-8455

Everglades City/Gulf Coast: In Florida, 1-800-445-7724; U.S.

1-800-233-1821
Marine Patrol: 305-743-6542
Coast Guard: 305-664-3141
Key Largo Information: 305-451-1414; 1-800-822-1088
Islamorada Information: 305-664-4503
Marathon Information: 305-743-5417
Lower Keys Information: 305-872-2411
Key West Information: 305-294-2587
Weather: Miami area, 305-661-5065; Key West, 305-296-2011
Customs: Miami area, 305-536-4126; Key West, 305-296-4700

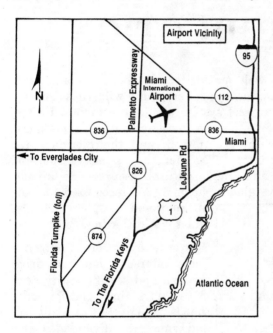

ADDITIONAL INFORMATION

Florida Keys
P.O. Box 1147
Key West FL 33041
Phone: US: 1-800-FLA-KEYS;
from outside the US
305-296-3811

Everglades National Park
Box 279
Homestead FL 33030
Phone: 305-247-6211

INTRODUCTION

Two worlds of beauty welcome visitors to the Everglades and Florida Keys—North America's last remaining wilderness swamp and the only living coral reef system off the continental United States. The area encompasses five national parks—Everglades, Big Cypress, Biscayne, Fort Jefferson, and the Florida Keys National Marine Sanctuary. Together they preserve some of America's most valued and unique natural resources. So unique, in fact, that the Everglades have been recognized as an International Biosphere Reserve and a World Heritage Site.

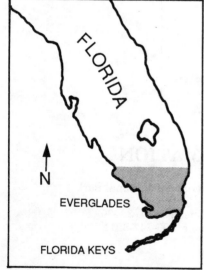

With the exception of offshore Fort Jefferson, you can drive through and see the entire area in two days' time, and for some that is enough. But to really see and enjoy the Everglades you must get out on the water, entertain some fish with a line and lure, paddle a canoe, take a boat tour, slosh along the swamp trails, see an alligator or a manatee, and squish some wet mud between your toes. During summer, mosquitos will bite you no matter what.

In the Keys, you must get salt water under your skin, breathe salt air into your lungs, taste some Key lime pie, and learn about the undersea world which attracts visitors from around the world.

EVERGLADES

The Everglades region is a great wilderness. It is a freshwater river which flows across most of the southern tip of the Florida peninsula. Just six inches deep and 50 miles wide, it originates at Lake Okeechobee in the north and moves southward to the Gulf of Mexico. The Indians call it "Pa-hay-okee", the river of grass, for the dense prairies of razor-toothed sawgrass which grow from the river.

Everglades, River of Grass is the classic book on the area. Written in 1947 by Marjory Stoneman Douglas, a celebrated environmentalist, it was the first published work which brought attention to the need for conservation education.

Geographically, the Everglades region is loosely defined but generally thought of as the entire wet wilderness area south of Lake Okeechobee, an area of over seven million acres that encompasses Everglades National Park, Great Cypress National Park, Indian villages along Tamiami Trail, the Corkscrew Swamp Sanctuary, a National Audubon Society refuge, Collier-Seminole State Park, and the Fakahatchie Preserve. The area is bounded by resort cities on the east coast and fringed by a maze of mangrove islands which rise from the Gulf of Mexico on its south and western shores. For visitors, the Everglades exert a primitive sort of magnetism.

Everglades National Park

Everglades National Park is just a small part of this watery expanse. Established in 1947, the park covers some 1.4 million acres. Despite the park's size, its environment is threatened by the disruptive activities of agriculture, industry and urban development in the surrounding area.

It is a quiet zone which, at first, seems nothing more than a wide

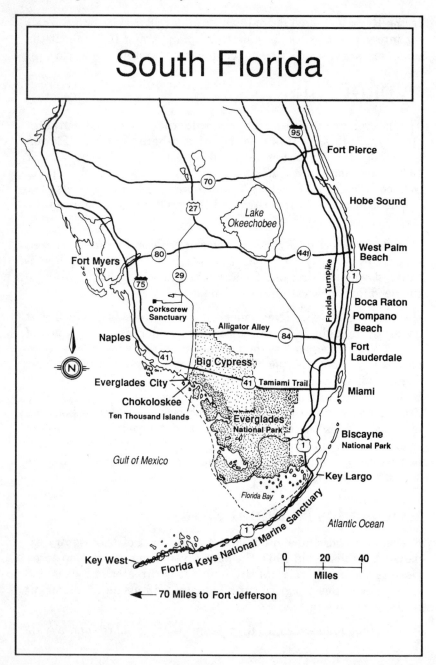

South Florida

expanse of sawgrass prairies and nagging insect life, until late fall when the omnipresent clouds of bugs leave. During this period, from mid-November through mid-March, the waterways and trails transform into a wilderness paradise for canoers, hikers, bird watchers, fishermen and campers. Along the hiking and canoe trails visitors come close-up to exotic wading birds and alligators in their natural habitat. In remote areas, crocodiles share the vast marshland with rare Florida panthers, and the gentle manatee—an aquatic, plant-eating mammal dubbed the "sea cow" for its huge proportions.

A dense network of mangrove islands lace the western Gulf shoreline thus creating a protected, coastal, water route—the Wilderness Waterway. Favored for rugged canoe-camping expeditions, the north end of the route begins at Everglades City and the Ten Thousand Island region. It winds through shallow creeks and bays to Flamingo, an outpost on Florida Bay, the south end of Everglades National Park.

Big Cypress National Preserve

Some consider Big Cypress National Preserve the "real Everglades" because it more closely resembles the Hollywood sets. Unlike other national parks, and despite environmentalists' concern, it is the one area where air-boats, swamp buggies and other off-road vehicles are allowed (by permit). Hunting and trapping continue. It is considered one of the best areas for fresh water fishing.

The Florida Trail, a marked hiking trail which runs through Big Cypress from Alligator Alley to the Tamiami Trail is often drier than the foot trails in Everglades National Park.

Hundreds of giant cypress trees once grew in Big Cypress. Today few remain. Those that do are 600 to 700 years old. Their bulbous bases flare downward and outward to root systems loosely locked in rich, wet organic peat. Their girths outstretch the combined embrace of you and three long-armed friends. Protected by the National Park Service since 1974, the Big Cypress trees stand safe from earlier fates as gutters, coffins, stadium seats, pickle barrels and the hulls of PT boats. Over 570,000 acres have been set aside as a National Preserve.

Broad belts of today's dwarf cypress edge wet prairies and line the sloughs. Cypress domes dot the horizon. Here, an occasional Florida panther leaves impressive paw marks in wet marl. Black bears claw crayfish from the sloughs, or rip cabbage palmetto apart for its soft fruits.

Eleven thousand acres of Big Cypress are owned by the Audubon Society. Known as the Corkscrew Swamp Sanctuary, this area is a breeding ground for the endangered wood stork.

Two major highways cross the Big Cypress Preserve, Alligator Alley (Rt. 84) and Tamiami Trail (U.S. 41). With Rt. 29 to the west, they enable you to explore the park which covers about 40 % of the Big Cypress Swamp. The best spots for nature photography and bird watching are from the boardwalk in the Corkscrew Swamp Sanctuary and the Loop Road (Rt. 94) from 40-Mile Bend to Monroe Station. But watch out for potholes and after a heavy rain the road may be impassable. A graded dirt road—Turner River Road (Rt. 839) connects Tamiami Trail and Alligator Alley. Expect these unpaved roads to be dusty or muddy and rough.

THE FLORIDA KEYS

The mangrove islands in the south sector of Everglades National Park drift across Florida Bay to the upper Florida Keys and Key Largo, the largest and northernmost of the inhabited islands. You need a boat to enter the Florida Keys from this direction, but can get there more easily from the eastern shore by car. The Florida Keys, from Key Largo to Key West, connect to the mainland and to each other by a cement and steel wonder—U.S. 1. The islands arc southwesterly toward Cuba and the Caribbean Sea.

Picturesque cycling paths, nature hikes, and flat-water canoe trails exist in the Keys also, but colorful living reefs which parallel the islands from Key Biscayne to Key West are the big attraction here. This area is known for diving, snorkeling, deep-sea fishing, and ocean cruising. In the lower keys (Big Pine to Key West),

Sea Turtle

ocean kayaks and shallow-draft sailboats are popular for snorkeling and shelling excursions to nearby out islands. Resorts, recreational facilities, restaurants, and shopping areas pave the way from Key Largo to Key West.

Biscayne National Park

Biscayne National Park, located just 21 miles east of Everglades National Park, was established as a national monument in 1968. In 1980 it was enlarged to 181,500 acres and designated as a national park. Most of it is underwater. The park boundaries start just below Key Biscayne and encompass the reefs, islands and subsea area from the mainland out to about 15 miles offshore. The south end tips the Key Largo National Marine Sanctuary. Biscayne encompasses the uninhabited northern section of Key Largo, Elliot Key, Sands Key, Boca Chita Key and some private islands to the north, the Ragged Keys. An ornamental lighthouse on Boca Chita Key marks that spot as a boater's favorite for picnics. The entire area is popular for ocean sports—canoeing, fishing, diving, snorkeling and wilderness camping. The Intracoastal Waterway runs through the park boundaries.

The islands can only be reached by boat. Free boat docks are located at Elliott Key harbor and University Dock. You must make reservations to moor overnight. Call 305-247-PARK.

The main north-south highways approaching Biscayne are Florida's Turnpike and U.S. 1. The most direct route to Convoy Point is North Canal Drive (S.W. 328 St.). U.S. 1 intersects North Canal in Homestead. Driving south on the turnpike you can reach North Canal by taking Tallahassee Rd. (S.W. 137 Ave.) south. Public boat tours leave from Convoy Point.

Florida Keys National Marine Sanctuary

Formed over thousands of years, the Florida Reef Tract is the largest coral reef system of the North American continent.

Corals are invertebrate animals made up of polyps living in a colony. Each polyp secretes a skeletal deposit that remains after death and provides the base on which the living polyps grow. This continuing process produces the exquisite floral patterns, giant boulders, jagged pillars and spires that are the magnificence of the coral reef.

The outlying reefs are functional, as well as beautiful. They help cement the foundation of the Florida Keys and form a critical breakwater that diffuses the energy of storm-driven waves. In addition, the coral reef is a prime source of sand for Florida's beaches. Fish nibbling on corals and calcareous algae produce more than 2.5 tons of sand per acre annually.

Future generations of visitors may expect to enjoy the continued pristine majesty of the Florida Keys' colorful living reefs thanks to a 1990 federal law designating the entire Keys island chain as a national marine sanctuary.

You can view the reefs via dive, snorkel or glass-bottom boat. Miles of reef fish and reef residents will line up to look you over. They will swim up to your mask (yes, even some big guys) and they will curiously peer back at you through the glass-bottom boat panes. They see one million divers per year, yet are still fascinated by our designer wetsuits, day-glo masks and gobs of gear. Leave the aerosol cheese and pepperoni slices at home though. Too many divers feeding unnatural things to the fish are causing them stomach disorders.

Key West

No visit to the lower end of Florida is complete without a visit to Key West, the southernmost city on the U.S. east coast. Long a haven for artists and writers, this island city exerts a charm all its own. For a long stay, it is perfect for mixing adventurous sports with cosmopolitan activities and accommodations. Sign up for a day of ocean kayaking, fly by seaplane to a remote snorkeling island, sail, windsurf, or deep-sea fish, and return in time for sunset watching—an applauded nightly ritual on the waterfront. On shore, there are museums to explore, rides on the Trolley and Conch Train, historic-home tours, shopping and palm-lined beaches.

If your visit is just a day's stop, view the entire city from atop the lighthouse, then below by foot, bicycle or moped.

Fort Jefferson National Monument

Almost 70 miles west of Key West lies a cluster of seven islands called the Dry Tortugas, which, along with surrounding coral reefs, shoals and waters, make up Fort Jefferson National Monument. You need to travel by seaplane or boat to visit the area. Boaters will find safe anchorage in the Tortugas harbor. Visitors to the national monument enjoy good fishing, snorkeling and touring the ruins of the historic fort.

Famous for bird and marine life, as well as for its legends of pirates and sunken gold, the central feature is Fort Jefferson itself, largest of the 19th-century American coastal forts.

ENVIRONMENT

Despite south Florida's lush appearance, water management—its quality, quantity, and distribution—is one of the most critical environmental issues facing the area today. A current population expansion of more than 350,000 new residents per year puts huge demands on the natural resources.

Throughout the 1900's grand schemes sought to drain vast regions: meandering rivers were gutted to straight canals; sawgrass prairies became sugarcane and citrus plantations. Loggers came. Oil rigs came. Land speculators descended. Then came roads, and drainage canals that parched extensive tracts. But the main resource turned out to be water and today Florida is much involved in environment protection efforts.

FARMING ALTERS THE NATURAL FLOW OF WATER

It is just in recent years that man has realized the enormous impact on the national parks and sanctuaries of what happens outside their boundaries.

The Everglades watershed originates in the central Florida Kissimmee River basin north of Lake Okeechobee. In the past, summer thunderstorms flooded this region, Lake Okeechobee, and extensive areas of Everglades marsh. This created a shallow, wide river which flowed slowly south through the Everglades to the mangrove estuaries of the Gulf of Mexico. The summer rains would then give way to a six-month dry season. Everglades plants and animals adapted to this seasonal wet/dry cycle.

Water runoff, now containing nutrients and pesticides from dairy and sugar cane farms around Lake Okeechobee, drains into the canals and wetlands—often detouring hundreds of miles through residential areas before what remains of it reaches the Everglades wilderness areas. After flowing through the marshlands, the chemically treated water eventually reaches the salt water bays.

An estimated 1.5 tons of phosphorus is dumped into Lake Okeechobee per day. This raises the levels of nitrates and phosphates to 20 times higher than the normally low amounts once found in the sanctuaries. Beneficial algae and oxygen-producing aquatic plants—the spawning ground for fish—are choked out by cattails which thrive in the nutrient-rich water.

Periods of drought are especially harmful. Huge demands from cities and farms lower the freshwater tables causing an infusion of salt water. This causes a rapid change in salinity levels which, combined with pollutants, drastically alters and in some cases eliminates the habitats of fish, birds and other wildlife. In 1989, fires devastated 400,000 acres of Everglades National Park.

When people and animals live closely it is usually the wildlife that suffers, but man also depends on the natural flow being restored. Much of the area's rainfall which fills the huge aquifers (natural underground reservoirs) depends on the wetlands staying wet. Talk of desalinization for drinking water could become a reality.

EFFECTS ON THE REEFS

In the ocean and salt-water bays the overabundance of nutrients produces algae blooms which choke out living corals and turtle grasses. Sea urchins which once kept the algae in check mysteriously died off during 1983. A demand for seafood has caused a large decline in algae-eating fish from over-harvesting.

WADING BIRD POPULATIONS DECLINE

The number of wading birds nesting in colonies (rookeries) in the southern Everglades region has declined from approximately 265,000 birds to 18,500 birds, a 93% reduction, since the 1930's. The endangered wood stork has declined from 6,000 nesting birds in the 1960's to 500 today. Of the remaining wading species, 70% have moved outside park boundaries to nest. Declines have been caused by changes in the water flow to Everglades National Park.

ENDANGERED SPECIES

There are eleven endangered species in the Everglades—the wood stork, snail kite, Cape Sable seaside-sparrow, Arctic peregrine falcon (a winter visitor), American crocodile, red-cockaded woodpecker, southern bald eagle, hawksbill turtle, green turtle, and Atlantic Ridley turtle, Florida panther, and the West Indian manatee. The survival of these species has been a major focus of the parks' research effort.

RECOVERY PROGRAMS

Recent Laws Bring New Hope for Survival

Recent laws have been passed to return the entire water flow of south Florida to a more natural state. The Dairy Rule of 1987 requires that runoff from pastures be directed into holding ponds by 1992. The Surface Water Improvement and Management Act requires pollution reduction and environmental controls by all water management districts. Proposals for huge tracts of farmland being used for pollution filtration may become reality.

Parks Play an Important Role

Giving park and marine sanctuary status to larger areas of the region has helped to protect the environment, fund research studies, and educate the public through the dissemination of literature, ranger-led tours and other activities.

Most of the private expeditions listed throughout this guide are oriented toward nature-study with an emphasis on ecological concerns.

The Corkscrew Swamp Sanctuary

In the mid-50's the Big Cypress Swamp was threatened by logging, drainage and development. This would have meant the destruction of the last remaining stands of mature bald cypress trees in the nation. Many of these towering giants are nearly 500 years old. Fortunately, conservationists initiated a fund-raising drive which saved 2,640 acres of the swamp. Today the Corkscrew Sanctuary is owned and operated by the National Audubon Society and encompasses approximately 11,000 acres. The sanctuary remains relatively undisturbed and has the largest colony of wood storks in the country.

The Manatee

The West Indian manatee, a large gray-brown, herbivorous, a-quatic mammal found in Florida's shallow coastal waters, canals, rivers and springs has become a highly endangered species. Population studies indicate that there may be as few as 1,200 manatees in Florida waters. Many are killed or severely injured by power boats. Habitat destruction puts these docile creatures in jeopardy.

Manatees are protected by the Marine Mammal Protection Act of 1972, the Endangered Species Act of 1973 and the Florida Manatee Sanctuary Act of 1978. It is illegal to harass, harm, pursue, hunt, shoot, wound, kill, annoy or molest manatees.

To report manatee deaths, injuries, harassment or radio-tagged manatees call the Florida Marine Patrol at 1-800-DIAL- FMP.

Rescue and Rehabilitation Program

After the Marine Mammal Protection Act of 1972 and the Endangered Species Act of 1973 were passed, marine specialists at

Sea World were approached to aid in the rescue of beached or stranded marine mammals. In cooperation with the Department of the Interior, the National Marine Fisheries Service, the Florida Department of Natural Resources and the Florida Marine Patrol, Sea World developed the Beached Animal Rescue and Rehabilitation Program in 1973. Since that time, animal care specialists have responded to hundreds of calls to aid sick, injured or orphaned manatees, dolphins, whales, otters, sea turtles and a variety of birds. The marine life park bears all costs of the rescue program, including those for research, transportation and rehabilitation.

As a result of research conducted by Sea World's animal husbandry staff in aviculture, animal care and aquarium departments, valuable baseline data is being established and shared with scientists worldwide. Food preferences, responses to antibiotic therapy, the safest transportation equipment and the swiftest rescue techniques have been documented by the staff. This data is invaluable in the effort to protect marine mammals from extinction. Sea World is the largest of the two facilities in the state that are authorized to rescue, care for and release manatees.

Boaters and Divers Can Help the Manatee

• Wear polarized glasses while operating a boat. Polarized lenses make it much easier to see the "swirling" that occurs when a manatee surfaces for air.

• Stay in the center of the marked channel. Channel depth reduces the likelihood of pinning or crushing manatees.

• Stay out of seagrasses. Grass beds are prime manatee habitat, including where hydrilla and water hyacinths are present.

• Reduced speeds give you greater maneuverability to avoid a manatee when you see one, and you'll also save gas.

• Observe all manatee speed zones and caution areas.

• Use snorkel gear when diving with manatees. The sound of bubbles from SCUBA gear can frighten the manatees.

• Manatees are wild animals and should not be fed. Close exposure to or dependence on humans can be harmful.

• A cow and her calf belong together. Please do not separate them. Do not separate or single out any individual manatee from a herd.

• Look, but please do not touch the manatee.

• Take only as many pictures as the manatees will voluntarily pose for.

Seabird Sanctuary

The Suncoast Seabird Sanctuary, founded by Ralph Heath, Jr., is home to permanently injured seabirds from all parts of the state who might otherwise be destroyed. Some find homes in zoos and tourist attractions. Many injured birds recover after treatment and are released. One common malady arises from fishermen's hooks getting caught in their beaks. Some birds who have gotten into trouble a second or third time have returned on their own for help. The Sanctuary is north of the Everglades on the beach at Indian Shores between St. Petersburg and Clearwater.

Dolphin Sanctuaries

Injured or ailing dolphins and those stressed out from performing in circuses and attractions are finding rest and retirement care at the Grassy Key Research Center, Theatre of the Sea, Islamorada and holding pens which are being set up in the Keys.

Reef Relief

Many factors, both natural and those caused by human intrusion, contribute to the destruction of a coral reef. Some relief has been gained by the mooring buoy system, one of the most effective programs to reduce anchor damage and to provide you with a convenient means of securing your boat in the sanctuary. The buoys are available on a first come, first served basis for everyone.

You can help protect the fragile coral by following the regulations and restrictions that apply to the Sanctuary:

• Do not allow your anchor, anchor chain or line to contact coral.

• Just touching coral causes damage to the fragile polyps; when diving, snorkeling or swimming on a reef do not allow your hands, knees, tank or fins to contact the coral.

• Spearfishing is not allowed.

• Hand feeding of the fish is discouraged.

• Corals, shells, starfish and other animals cannot be removed from the reefs.

• Regulations prohibiting littering and discharge of any substances except chum are strictly enforced.

• Fines are imposed for running aground or damaging coral.

• Historical artifacts are protected.

• The red and white dive flag must be flown while diving or snorkeling. Boats must go slow enough to leave no wake within 100 yards of a dive flag.

Information on National Oceanic and Atmospheric Administration Sanctuary Programs is available from NOAA/NOS/OCRM, 3300 Whitehaven St., N.W., Washington D.C. 20235.

For additional information on the Everglades write to the Superintendent of Everglades National Park, Box 279, Homestead FL 33030.

Great white heron, Key Largo

Seaplanes at Fort Jefferson

HISTORY

Not long after Christopher Columbus discovered the New World in 1492, adventurer Ponce de Leon and fellow Spanish chronicler Antonio de Herrera sighted the Florida Keys. That was Easter Sunday, May 15, 1513.

Herrera wrote for posterity: "To all this line of islands and rock islets they gave the name of Los Martires because the rocks as they rose to view appeared like men who were suffering; and the name remained fitting because of the many that have been lost there since."

The name Florida was later chosen from the Spanish name for Easter: Pascuas Florida.

Florida remained under Spanish rule until 1763 when the British captured Havana and traded it for Florida. By 1783 it was back under Spanish rule.

THE INDIANS

The Calusa and Tekesta Indians first populated the southern Everglades and the Keys. To the north were the Seminoles and Miccosukees.

Word of Bahama natives being carried from their homeland and forced into slavery by the white man prepared the Calusas to fiercely defend their freedom. Early attempts by the Spaniards to settle in the Keys were met with the sting of arrows. In 1521, a band of Calusas in primitive canoes attacked approaching

Roseate spoonbill

Spaniards. Among those struck down was Ponce de Leon when an arrow pierced his suit of armor. He later died in Havana. Wars between the Indians and the white man raged on for centuries. Many of the original Indian tribes died off from white man's diseases; some were taken into slavery by the Spaniards and moved to Cuba and other areas of the Caribbean.

Many runaway black slaves sought refuge in the Everglades and were taken in by the Indians. This along with border disputes fueled the Indian battles with the U.S.

In 1817 U.S. troops led by Andrew Jackson forced most of the Indians to reservations in the West. One tribe, the Seminoles, never surrendered to U.S. forces.

In 1818, under President Thomas Jefferson's leadership, the U.S. bought Florida for five million dollars. Descendents of the Seminoles and the Miccosukees still populate the Everglades region. Both tribes descend from the Creek Indians who migrated from Georgia in the early 1700's.

Early Indians were hunters, fishermen and farmers. In the Everglades they built huge islands of shells. Many of these mounds still exist and are protected in Everglades National Park as historic preserves. Chokoloskee in the northwest Everglades area is one such island which has been paved over and made into an RV camp.

PIRATES

In the years following Ponce de Leon's first sighting, many Spanish and British vessels cruising the Florida straits became targets of piracy—first by the Indians, later by notorious figures like Henry Morgan, Blackbeard, Black Caesar, and Lafitte.

Not until Florida became part of the United States in 1821 were the pirates finally driven out.

FORTS

After 1821 military officials recognized the strategic importance of the Dry Tortugas. The nation that occupied the islands, U.S. officials realized, would control navigation of the Gulf.

Fort Jefferson was built with eight-foot-thick walls that rise 50 feet high. It has three gun tiers designed for 450 guns.

The fort was never fired upon, but during the Civil War it served as a military prison for captured deserters. For almost 10 years after the fighting stopped, it remained a prison. Among the prisoners sent here in 1865 were four of the so-called "Lincoln conspirators"—Michael O'Loughlin, Sammuel Arnold, Edward Spangler, and Dr. Samuel Mudd—who had been tried and convicted of complicity in the assassination of Abraham Lincoln. The most famous of these was Dr. Mudd, a Maryland physician who, knowing nothing of Lincoln's murder, had set the broken leg of the fugitive assassin, John Wilkes Booth. Sentenced to life imprisonment, Mudd was pardoned in 1869 for helping to fight the 1867 yellow fever epidemic that struck the fort, felling 270 of the 300-man garrison and resulting in 38 fatalities.

The cell occupied by Dr. Mudd during his years of confinement can still be seen at the fort today.

It took 21 years—from 1854 to 1866—of hard labor, hurricanes and yellow fever epidemics to build the trapezoid-shaped Fort Zachary Taylor on Key West. During the Civil War, the Union controlled the fort on the island with strong local support. Fort Taylor was the home base for a successful blockade of Confederate ships, and some historians say the blockade cut a year off the War between the States. Two more Key West forts, East and West Martello Towers were authorized by Congress in 1844 to protect Fort Taylor from enemy attack, but neither was ever completed. Fort Taylor is believed to hold the largest number of Civil War artifacts in the nation and has become a major archaeological treasure.

WRECKING

The absence of lighthouses and reliable charts made early ocean travel hazardous in the shallow waters surrounding the Florida Keys. During storms many ships crashed on the reefs and became prey to wreckers who often killed all aboard for possible treasure.

By the 1830's a bit more law and order prevailed and a somewhat more civilized type of salvaging became a lucrative business, though some say the ships were still deliberately lured ashoal. Non-farming settlers in Key West and at Islamorada became wreckers and Key West became the wealthiest city in the infant United States Republic from the bounty of that profitable industry. The construction of lighthouses and lighted marker towers on the reefs put an eventual end to the wrecking business. Carysfort Light was the first of the navigational beacons.

In 1960, remains of one 1733 treasure ship, the *San Pedro*, were discovered in Hawk Channel under 18 feet of water. Documents state that the 287-ton Dutch-built ship was carrying 16,000 pesos in Mexican silver and numerous crates of Chinese porcelain when she wrecked almost a half-league from Indian Key. Her discovery led to the recovery of small silver coins dated between 1731 and 1733, as well as cannons trapped under the ballast pile. Today the site is protected as an underwater archaeological preserve and utilized as a tour for snorkelers.

Key West Lighthouse

FARMING, SHARK SKINS, PLUME HUNTING AND CIGARS

In 1822 Key West became the first permanent settlement. Spaniards who first set foot on the islands found piles of bones and thus named it Island of Bones or Cayo Hueso; a name which later became Anglicized into Key West.

Early settlers farmed productive groves of Key limes, tamarind and breadfruit. In the lower Keys pineapple farms flourished and a large pineapple factory was built which furnished canned pineapple to most of Eastern North America. As transportation and refrigeration improved, Hawaiian plantations took over the pineapple market.

In later years, a thriving shark factory was established on Big Pine Key amidst the abandoned farms. It hired workers to catch sharks and the hides were skinned, salted down, and sent north to the home factory in New Jersey to be processed into a tough leather called shagreen. This abrasive skin was used by cabinet makers for sandpaper.

In the 1870's women's fashion dictated the use of huge feathers in their hats. Plume hunting grew to huge proportions in the Everglades. Greedy hunters ravaged the nesting grounds of egrets and herons killing thousands of birds to sell to the millinery trade. Desperate to stop the slaughter, the Audubon Society sent game wardens to protect the rookeries. Finally, the public took notice when newspapers covered the death of Guy Bradley, a game warden murdered by the plume hunters. By 1890 the bird population was badly depleted, but national publicity about the murder raised public concern and brought an end to plume hunting.

Still later, cigar makers from Cuba established factories in Key West. By 1880 over 100 million cigars were produced. Labor problems later forced the industry to Tampa.

THE SPANISH-AMERICAN WAR

Key West took on historic importance when its harbor served as a port to warships during the Spanish-American War. Though

Tampa was the principal base for military activity, the Key West Navy Yard, just 90 miles from Havana, became a jump off point for hospital and supply ships. At a special memorial in the Key West cemetery rest the bodies of those who died when the U.S. battleship *Maine* was sunk in Havana's Harbor in 1898, the event which touched off the Spanish-American War.

FLAGLER'S RAILROAD

In 1903, railroad tycoon Henry Flagler built his impossible railroad "that went to sea" on which wealthy visitors travelled to vacation in the Keys. The railroad connected existing rail service from Homestead to Key West and to Cuba by sea-going ferries which carried the cars across the Gulf. On Labor Day in 1935, a nameless hurricane ravaged the Keys with 200-mph winds and an 18-foot tidal surge which ripped out huge caissons the railroad builders had constructed to connect the islands. Though most of the bridges held up, the railbeds on the lowlands were destroyed. They were never rebuilt. Sections of the old railroad bridges remain and can be seen in the lower Keys.

In the depression years the Keys faced a bleak future. The city of Key West went bankrupt.

It was then, with Federal aid, Keys officials decided that they still had something to offer—sea, sun and a good winter climate. In this somewhat weather-beaten, shabby gentility of the 1930s, the idea of a highway to replace the railroad was born. The famed Florida Keys Overseas Highway (U.S. 1) opened in 1938. Three years later World War II dashed all the prospects of tourist gold.

The U.S. Navy came to the rescue again to build a submarine base in Key West. Shrimp were discovered—the Keys now vital pink gold—and, following the war, the tourists finally began to come in earnest.

THE TAMIAMI TRAIL

Most of the western Everglades region remained largely unexplored until 1915 when construction of the Tamiami Trail began. Workmen were plagued by mosquitos, and snakes.

The Maine *Monument, Key West*

Many deaths resulted from snakebites and related fungus infections. Armed guards were eventually hired to shoot the snakes. A good portion of the roadbed was built on wet mud which often caused the heavy machinery to sink or fall over. Completion seemed impossible. Work crews endured despite the hardships and the 120-mile road linking Miami to Tampa was dedicated on April 26, 1928.

With the completion of the Tamiami Trail and, in 1938, the first Overseas Highway from the mainland to Key West, commercialization of the area began. Tourism and land development have since boomed.

AERIAL TOURS

Perhaps the most intriguing view of the Everglades and Florida Keys can be enjoyed from the air. Offshore you'll climb over a rainbow of coral. To the north, flights along the 100-mile Wilderness Waterway between Everglades City and Flamingo offer breathtaking views of vast marshlands and the varied plant communities which thrive there. West of Everglades City, in the Ten Thousand Islands region, you'll see narrow waterways twist and turn into a mosaic of exotic shapes.

At low altitude, you may spot the silhouette of a manatee or a huge alligator slithering beneath the water's surface.

If light plane tours are a new addition to your adventure list, book a morning flight on a day with calm winds. Rising columns of air which cause light aircraft to bounce a bit are more prevalent as afternoon sun heats the ground. Winds, if gusting, may also cause a bumpy ride.

Be sure to bring binoculars and a camera.

THE EVERGLADES AND KEY LARGO

Bob Barnes, chief pilot of Key Largo Air Service, offers 50- and 80-minute sightseeing flights over the Everglades, Key Biscayne National Park and the area from Key Largo to Key West. Rates start at $59 (minimum two people) for a ride in a four-seat Cessna. See all three regions for $110. Larger groups board a Twin Piper

Aztec or Navajo Chieftain. Bob has developed an informational tape for each region which is played in flight. Custom sightseeing charters (rates by the hour) may be booked for other destinations. For additional information write to Key Largo Air Service, P.O. Box 519, Homestead FL 33030. Phone: 1-800-628-3610; in Florida, 305- 248-1100.

MARATHON

Keys Air offers long or short light-plane sightseeing tours to any point in the Keys. Rates vary with air time. Book a flight at Marathon Airport. Phone 305-743-3700. In Florida, 1-800-AIR WING.

KEY WEST
By Seaplane

Foremost in out-island tour popularity are half-day seaplane excursions to Fort Jefferson in the Dry Tortugas. Located 70 miles west of Key West, the fort is the most inaccessible National Monument in the western hemisphere. The islands, thoroughly off the beaten path, were named for their lack of fresh water and once-abundant turtle population. Today, prime attractions are the spectacular snorkeling found on the surrounding coral reefs and a chance to explore the historic, hexagonal, brick fort where Dr. Samuel Mudd was imprisoned for his alleged part in the assassination of President Lincoln.

On the flight out you'll spot numerous shipwrecks and the treasure site of Spanish galleons, *Atocha* and *Margarita*. When the sea is calm the clear waters of the Gulf magnify an outline of the wrecks. Flights can be booked through the Key West Seaplane Base for a morning or afternoon departure.

There are restrooms on the island, but no food or beverage service facilities. You must bring everything with you. And while plans to add a picnic lunch or possibly a beach barbecue to the seaplane itinerary are in the works, at this writing passengers are advised to pack their own snacks and cold beverages.

The flight time ranges from 30 to 40 minutes. The planes, float-equipped Cessnas, carry up to five passengers. Cost is presently $120 per person (price may fluctuate).

The seaplane base, located on Stock Island, is open year round. To reach it turn right onto Junior College Road from the southbound lane of U.S. 1. The turnoff is just before the bridge to Key West. There is a sign on Junior College Road which directs you left to the base. To reserve a seat, phone: 305-294-6978. Fax: 305-292-1091. All flights are weather-dependent and take place only during daylight hours. Free snorkeling gear is available.

ABOUT FORT JEFFERSON

Situated on Garden Key, the immense 50-ft-high fort was once considered a strategic point for controlling navigation through the Gulf. Construction of the brick and stone fort was started in 1846, and, although work continued for almost 30 years, little was done after 1866. Updated weaponry introduced during the war, particularly the rifled cannon, had made the fort obsolete. Moreover, in 1864 engineers discovered that the fort's foundations rested not upon a solid coral reef as originally thought, but upon sand and coral boulders washed up by the sea. As the huge structure settled the eight-foot-thick walls began to crack.

Though never a target of military action, the fort served as a prison for Civil War deserters and periodically as an anchorage for the American naval fleet. The Army abandoned the fort in 1874 following a damaging hurricane and an outbreak of yellow fever. In 1935, President Franklin D. Roosevelt rescued the fort from oblivion and proclaimed the area a national monument.

By Open Cockpit

For a romantic tour of Old Key West, hop into the front seat of an open-cockpit biplane. Bring a friend; it seats two. The pilot rides in the back. Helmets and goggles supplied.

Fred Cabanas, chief pilot and owner of Island Aeroplane Tours, offers a wide range of scenic flights. Choose a ride over south-shore

beaches and island resorts; or a view of Mallory Square and Old
Town Key West; an island shipwreck excursion which takes you
over Channel West of Fleming Key; or combine them all with a
coral-reef tour. Fred's "See-it-All" tour starts with flying over a
visual maze of coral reefs, then heads west to Boca Grand Island
(13 miles west of Key West), over Woman Key, Man Key and
Ballast Key. The over-ocean flights offer excellent photo
opportunities. Passengers often spot sharks, rays and migrating
schools of fish. Rates vary from approximately $50 to $150
depending on air time and are apt to fluctuate.

Ace aerial photographer, Rebecca Whitley offers spectacular
air-to-air color shots of your flight for an additional fee. This must
be arranged well in advance, though. All flights depart Key West
International Airport. Island Aeroplane Tours is just off South
Roosevelt Boulevard at Key West Airport. Call 305-294-TOUR for
reservations.

Sunny-side Down

If flying over the ocean in an antique biplane isn't adventure
enough, tighten your leather helmet and goggles for the
ultimate—an aerobatic ride in a Pitts S-2A. You've always wanted
to be a stunt pilot? Great! Take a lesson. That's inverted, of
course. For a moment the ocean becomes the sky, and the sky the
sea below. Do this before lunch. Dangerous? You wanted
adventure! Reticent companions can relax in knowing the
aerobatic flights are single-passenger only. And instructor-pilot
Fred Cabanas flies 3,500 passengers a year, holds an Air
Transport rating and is currently training his eleven-year-old
daughter Kelly to fly the Pitts. Also at Island Aeroplane Tours.
Rates for an aerobatic ride start at $110. For a lesson, $150 per
hour. Phone: 305-294-TOUR.

For the Traditionalist

Flights in a standard, high-wing, four-seat Cessna are offered by
Island City Flying Service at Key West International Airport.
While these flights may not provide quite the romance and

Seagull

adventure of waterflying or barnstorming in an open-cockpit, the
view is still splendid and the price tag a bit lower; in the front seat
you can open the window and take pictures. Aim straight down to
keep the wing strut out of the shot. You can also arrange for a
night flight over the city. Rates start at $40. Flying lessons are of-
fered too. For reservations phone: 305-296-8895.

BOAT TOURS

ROYAL TOURS ABOARD THE *AFRICAN QUEEN*

Half-hour cruises on the *African Queen* are offered by owner/historian, James Hendricks. Tours depart from the Holiday Inn docks (MM 100).

Powered by the original engine, the *Queen* lets off steam as the first mate sounds the fog horn and pulls away from the dock. The ride is wonderful as is the captain's photo journal which is passed around during the tour. It includes notes to Hendricks from Katherine Hepburn, foreign dignitaries, and photos from his European, Canadian, Australian and US tours. Upon return, passengers are given honorary *African Queen* captain licenses and a postcard of her for remembrance.

Hendricks, dubbed the "jovial millionaire" by southern journalists, is indeed aglow as he shares his prized possession with guests. He purchased the vessel in 1982 and restored her as close as possible to original. Hendricks is the only licensed captain for the coal-powered steam vessel and is a delight to join on this special adventure. Cost: $15. Call ahead to reserve a seat. Phone: 305-451-4655.

AIRBOAT RIDES

Originally designed for hunting, airboats are now used for sightseeing the sawgrass prairies and mangrove thickets along the Tamiami Trail. Sign up for an exhilarating ride at Wootens (813-695-2781) on US 41 in Everglades City. Experienced guides navigate the fan-driven crafts along old Indian canoe trails. Nearer to Miami, also on 41, you can arrange for a ride at the Miccosukee Indian Village.

The African Queen

Phone: 305-223-8388 weekends, 305-223-8380 weekdays. Sightseeing trips last 30 minutes and cost $10.

Despite popularity with tourists, airboats are not allowed within Everglades National Park boundaries. The noise frightens wildlife and disrupts endangered species nesting grounds.

EVERGLADES NATIONAL PARK TOURS

Scenic boat tours through the Ten Thousand Islands region are arranged at the Everglades National Park, Gulf Ranger Station on Chokoloskee Causeway. The two and one-half hour, ranger-guided trip has a brief stop for shelling on Kingston Key, a small island on the edge of the Gulf. Frequent sightings of porpoise, manatees, eagles, nesting ospreys, and roseate spoonbills are reported. Schedules of departure times and prices are posted at the concession office and on the bulletin board at the Gulf Coast Ranger Station. Phone: 800-445-7724 or 813-695-2591 for additional information. Write Everglades National Park Boat Tours, P.O. Box 119 ,Everglades, FL 33929.

Similar tours through Florida Bay depart the Flamingo marina (305-253-2241.)

GLASS BOTTOM BOAT TOURS

Glass bottom boat tours are entertaining and educational. They offer a long look at the living reefs which parallel the Florida Keys from Key Biscayne to KeyWest. Most of the boats have rest rooms, a snack bar and go out most days of the year.

Biscayne National Underwater Park, Inc. operates a 53-foot glass bottom boat in Biscayne National Park, a coral reef area which stretches from the southern tip of Key Biscayne to the northern tip of Key Largo. As boats pass over the shallow reefs, visitors get a look at submerged WWII aircraft wrecks inhabited by huge nurse sharks, angel fish, turtles, spiny lobster, parrot fish and schools of grunts and sargeant majors. The boats depart Convoy Point. Be sure to phone ahead to confirm schedule. Most days trips depart 10:00 am and 1:30 pm. Phone: 305-247-2400.

In Key Largo, one especially good trip is aboard the *San Jose* at John Pennekamp State Park. The two-hour excursion brings you eight miles out to Molasses Reef, an area favored by divers for its mazes of coral canyons and fish life.

The boat's seating area for the above-water portion of the tour is quite high and enables you to view nesting Cormorants eye-to-eye at the channel markers. It also allows for a fine aerial view of winding cuts and trails laced into the mangroves as a narrator points out nesting spots for osprey, herons, kingfishers or roseate spoonbills.

After passing through the mangrove channels of South Sound Creek to your left, you can see mud flats which are a feeding area for hundreds of wading birds. The birds are attracted by the edible debris and silt that collects on the shallow bar.

The *San Jose* and *Key Largo Princess*, another deluxe, glass bottom boat which operates from nearby Holiday Inn docks, have air-conditioned salons which are especially desirable during summer months. As the boat slithers through the coral canyons which form the reef, you are inches away from swaying lavender seafans, walls of curious grunts, and angel fish. A fierce-looking barracuda may come up and look back at you as you pass through a profusion of bubbles. As the boat glides through mazes of antler, staghorn and brain corals the narrator points out mating wrasses, neon parrotfish and other curious reef residents.

Crew members of the *San Jose* tell us the two things passengers ask to see are sharks and turtles. Sharks are a rare sight on the Pennekamp reefs, but turtles are seen on half of the trips. Queen and French angels, barracuda, parrotfish, wrasses, schools of grunts, and moray eels are more commonly seen.

Groups may book a private tour through John Pennekamp Park, on which you first see the reef through the viewing salon, then move to a shallow reef for snorkeling. Phone: 305-451-1621. Or write to Coral Reef Park Co., P.O. Box 1560, Key Largo FL 33037. (Handicapped-access).

Similar Pennekamp Park tours are offered aboard the *Key Largo Princess*, a 70-foot, glass bottom, aluminum motor yacht. It carries 125 passengers and is tied down at the Holiday Inn Docks, MM 100, Key Largo FL. Phone: 305-451-4655.

In Key West, glass bottom trips aboard the *Discovery* leave from the foot of Margaret St. at the Half Shell Raw Bar. The tour is two hours. The narration combines the colorful waterfront history of Key West and points of interest on the living coral reef

Call ahead to book a sunset or day cruise on the *Discovery*. Phone: 305-293-0099.

Glass bottom/snorkeling excursions off Key West are offered by Lange's Coral Princess fleet. Located at the end of Front Street, there are two trips daily, all gear and instruction included. Phone: 305-296-3287.

Note: If you are prone to motions sickness, take preventative measures before leaving the dock. The slow rocking motion of the boats crossing the reefs is the cause of most mal-de-mer.

SUNSET TOURS

In Key Largo, sunset tours depart the Quay Beach Club (MM 102) nightly. These bay cruises visit Bird Island, home to many pelicans, herons and ibis. Bring binoculars. Refreshments are available for purchase on this one and one-half hour tour.

Sail off into the sunset on Key West's own tall ship, the Schooner *Wolf*. This 74-foot, two-masted schooner departs the Key West Bight Marina at the foot of William Street for daily snorkel trips and romantic sunset cruises. Rates from$25. Phone: 305-296-WOLF (9653).

LIVEABOARDS AND BAREBOATING

Groups as small as six can charter a 50-foot sailing yacht for a week, complete with captain and cook for under $1000 per person. Trips are custom suited to your group for diving, snorkeling or simply relaxing. Most of the charter operators offer training too.

If you are an experienced sailor or boater you can charter a 30-foot or larger sail or motor yacht starting from about $1000 for seven days.

Atlantic Coast

Captain Danny Valls
Cruzan Yacht Charters

P.O. Box 53

Coconut Grove FL 33133

1-800-628-0785

Cruzan offers a large selection of O'Day, Watkins, Hunter and Sunward sailing yachts from 30 ' to 50'. Sample rate for an all-inclusive week for party of six aboard a 50' crewed Sunward would start at $5,200.

Treasure Harbor Marine, Inc
200 Treasure Harbor Drive

Islamorada FL 33036

1-800-FLA-BOAT

305-852-2458

Treasure Harbor Marine offers day sailboats and live-aboards. Prices range from $110 per day for a 19' day sail to $330 for a 41' bareboat. By the week from $395 to $1595. Crews available.

Florida Keys Motoryachts
P.O. Box 456

Key Largo FL 33037

1-800-443-4667

305-451-2221

Motoryachts, houseboats, and sailboats—crewed or bareboat.

Witts End
Marina Del Mar Docks
MM 100
P.O. Box 625
Key Largo FL 33037
305-451-3354
Crewed charters aboard Witts End, a beautiful 51' ketch

On the Gulf Coast
Fort Myers Yacht Charters
14341 Port Comfort Road
Fort Myers FL 33908
813-466-1800
Captained, bareboat and lessons.

CANOE AND KAYAK TOURS AND EXPEDITIONS

Canoe and kayak tours bring you face to face with seabirds, fish, dolphins and other forms of wildlife in the Everglades and Florida Keys. Here shallow creeks, streams and mangrove trails permit access to wilderness where other boats can't go. In fact, powerboats are prohibited on many of the canoe trails. Backcountry wildlife tours can be short or long range, guided or self-guided and as adventurous as you want them to be. Prices start at $25 for short tours and from $100 per day for week-long expeditions.

The marked trails in Florida's Keys (from Key Largo to Key West) are recommended for beginners. If you are new to paddling, the canoe and kayak renters will give you a short lesson and demonstration in basic paddling skills and safety. Ultimately, you must determine your own skill level and plan your own adventure accordingly. Non-arduous canoeing in unpopulated waters can also be done year-round in Biscayne National Aquatic Park, just south of Miami.

Winds and tides are the most important factors in planning your paddling tour. Tides can create strong currents. First-time canoe or kayak renters should stick to short protected trails. Let someone on shore know where you're going and how long you expect to be out. Don't over-estimate your abilities or under-estimate the elements. Begin all your trips into the wind, allowing an easier trip home.

FLORIDA KEYS CANOE AND KAYAK TRAILS

One of the more popular spots for paddling is a three-mile wilderness canoe trail at John Pennekamp State Park. Located on Key Largo at MM 102.5, this trail is an excellent choice for beginners. The waters are calm, the trails are well-marked, and they are off-limits to powerboats and sheltered by dense walls of mangrove trees. Swimming is safe, but better from the nearby park beaches. It is truly a tranquil setting for an afternoon's paddling adventure. You may encounter some current, but it is usually very light. The park has changing facilities, rest rooms, two beaches, shaded picnic and camping areas.

Wildlife photography opportunities abound. Brown pelicans glide gracefully overhead as diving cormorants and great white herons stalk the shore for food fish. Ducks will swim right up to your canoe and flying fish may surprise you by skimming the surface alongside your bow. In winter, the lovely, pink roseate spoonbill may be spotted in the mangrove shrubs along the trail. The water is crystal clear allowing a good look at French and queen angel fish, barracuda, parrot fish, and an occasional manatee.

Weather permitting, rentals and guided canoe trips are available. Canoes and tikis (small kayaks) rent for a low hourly rate. You must be at least 18 years old in Florida to sign for a rental. Write to Coral Reef Park Co., P.O. Box 1560, Key Largo FL 33037. Phone: in Florida 305-451-1621 or 800-432-2871; outside of Florida 800-344-8175.

The shallow flats of Long Key State Recreational Area, MM 67.5, are another protected paddling area. The mangrove swamps support a huge wading-bird population and an abundance of marine life. In fact, the island was once home to the Long Key Fishing Club, a mecca for the world's greatest saltwater fishermen until its destruction by a hurricane in 1935. During the winter months, park rangers offer programs on the ecology of the area. Canoe rentals available. Write Long Key State Recreation Area, P.O. Box 776, Long Key FL 33001; phone 305-664-4815.

Relaxing guided wildlife tours to and around the mangrove islands off Key West are offered by Key West Kayak Company and Mosquito Coast Kayaks . Your tour guide will explain the natural and cultural history, such as how the red mangrove formed the Keys and the tidal creeks between the Gulf and the Atlantic. Birds, sponges, coral and crustaceans will be identifed. You may chase a four-foot nurse shark or a sting ray in shallow water. Your guide will also teach you how to get in and out of your kayak so you can snorkel and explore a small secluded coral reef, or show you how to sail in a 15 mph wind with a large kite. Select from a two-hour trip to Pelican Island, a unique seabird habitat, backcountry tours, or ocean tours to secluded beaches where you can snorkel, picnic and beachcomb. Key West Kayak Tours depart daily at 9 am and 3 pm from the Geiger Key Marina beach. They include use of a stable, lightweight one- or two-person kayak and transportation to and from the departure location. The sea kayaks are longer and wider than whitewater kayaks and rudder controls are available. A double kayak is over 18 feet long. Spray skirts are eliminated, allowing the occupants to remain cool and comfortable. Write Key West Kayak Company, P.O. Box 4411, Key West FL 33041; phone 305-294-6494. Or Mosquito Coast Kayaks, 1107 Duval St., Key West FL; phone 305-294-7178.

Kayak rentals are available from Gulf Watersports, 2401 N. Roosevelt Boulevard; phone 305-296-1248.

A new area gaining popularity for canoeing is Biscayne National Park, consisting of 181,500 acres of pristine mangrove shorelines, islands, bays and offshore coral reefs. Most canoeing is along the southern shores of Biscayne Bay near park headquarters (U.S. 1 & S.W. 328th St.). Daily rentals of 17-foot, four-passenger Grumman aluminum canoes with paddles and life jackets are available from Biscayne Aqua-Center, Inc. For reservations phone 305-247-2400 or write to Captain Ed Davidson at P.O. Box 1270, Homestead FL 33030.

EVERGLADES NATIONAL PARK CANOE TOURS

Everglades National Park is a much more rugged environment for canoeing and kayaking than the Florida Keys, but perfect for those who want a true wilderness adventure. Here experienced canoe and kayak enthusiasts can combine paddling with superb fly fishing and backcountry camping. If you are new to canoe and kayak paddling, this is not the place to learn on your own. Gain experience by joining a guided-tour group. The presence of alligators, crocodiles and murky water makes swimming and wading, by intent or accident, unsafe. Seasonal low water and high mosquito levels can ruin even a short trip. Before going out on long trails you must be competent at marine navigation, and have a working knowledge of weather patterns, tides and currents in the area. The season is from early November through the end of April. Summer storms and a ferocious mosquito population take over the park from May through October.

Before embarking on any Everglades paddling tours be sure to file a float plan 24 hrs in advance with the park rangers and ask for a current trail condition report. This will advise you of current water and mosquito levels. Pre-trip advisories are crucial, especially during dry winter months when water levels in spots may drop to less than an inch leaving you in waist-deep mud.

There is an inland water route from Everglades City on the Gulf of Mexico to Flamingo on Florida Bay. Sequentially numbered markers guide you over its 99 miles. The route known as the Wilderness Waterway twists through expansive marine and estuarine areas of the park. These areas harbor almost every type of marine organism found in the Caribbean and serve as spawning grounds and nurseries for many of them. Larger creatures such as water birds, sea turtles, many types of fish sought by fishermen, and the endangered manatee are attracted to these waters because of their abundant food supplies. The route requires a minimum of seven days by canoe and a small motor is recommended. Primitive campsites are available along the route. Backcountry camping permits are required and may be

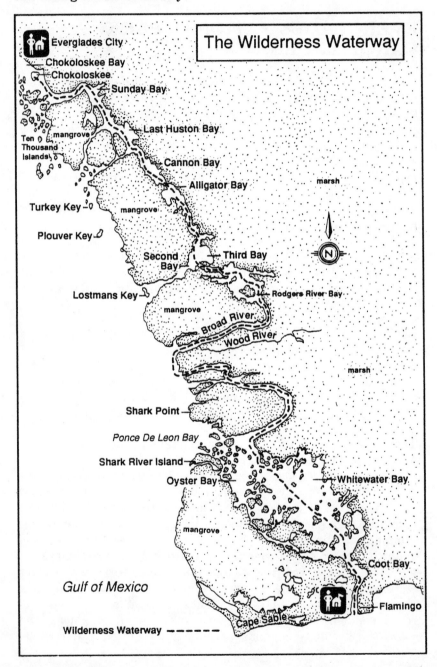

The Wilderness Waterway

obtained from the Everglades City or Flamingo ranger station. The permits are issued daily between 7:30 am and 4:00 pm. Charts 11430, 11432 and 11433 cover the area and are for sale at the main Visitor Center, Flamingo and in the Everglades City area.

Give plenty of space to power boats. In shallow areas they may not be able to come off a plane without hitting bottom. Stay to the right and turn your bow into their wake.

Canoe Camping

If you are canoe camping, carry at least one gallon of water per person per day. There is no freshwater in the backcountry. And be certain to bring trash bags. You must pack all your trash out with you. Food and water must be packed in hard shell containers. Raccoons will chew through plastic jugs and styrofoam coolers. Pets are not allowed in the backcountry or on the canoe trails.

Finding dry firewood is difficult. Bring a portable stove using compressed gas or liquid fuel.

Mosquitos and sand fleas can be overwhelming, particularly after a rainstorm. You'll need an ample supply of insect repellent and a tent with fine mesh screening. We found "Off—Deep Woods" repellent effective, but in extreme wet periods you are better off heading away from the marsh lands completely. The bug problem cannot be overemphasized. One canoe camper describes the mosquitos' arrival as follows: "You don't see them, you hear them coming. At first, I thought it was airplanes."

TEN THOUSAND ISLANDS DAY TRIPS

Trips within the Ten Thousand Islands sector originate at Everglades City on Chokoloskee Bay. You can rent a canoe at the Everglades National Park Boat Tours office or at North American Canoe Tours across the street, at Outdoor Resorts on Chokoloskee Island, or bring your own.

Put in at the canoe ramp next to the Ranger Station or next to Outdoor Resorts on Chokoloskee Island. Don't panic if you tip

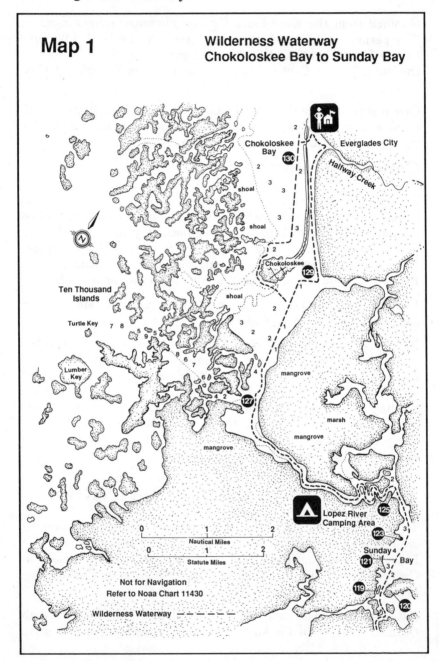

Map 1

**Wilderness Waterway
Chokoloskee Bay to Sunday Bay**

over. Chokoloskee Bay is shallow; it may be possible to walk to land. Be sure to have keys and valuables where they will not be lost in the water.

Time your trip so the tides help you. A falling tide flows toward the Gulf of Mexico; a rising tide flows toward the Ranger Station. If you have questions about handling a canoe, ask a ranger for assistance.

Sandfly Island Trip

Follow the marked channel south. Optional: circle the island in shallow water—you may have to walk your canoe across the oyster bar north of the island. Watch for strong tidal currents south of the island. The dock on Sandfly Island is two miles from the Ranger Station. There is a nature trail on Sandfly Island which features natural and cultural history. Estimated paddling time: 2.5 hours.

Chokoloskee Bay Loop

Follow the marked channel west, then south; turn east and follow the north margin of the Ten Thousand Islands to the other marked channel; turn north and follow the marked channel back to the Ranger Station. This trip is mostly open water with a few small mangrove islands not dependable for landing, especially at high tide. Estimated paddling time: 2.5 hours.

Collier Seminole State Park

Collier Seminole State Park is at Route 92 and the Tamiami Trail, about 17 miles west of Carnestown—the turnoff for Everglades City.

A limited number of visitors are allowed to visit this preserve each day by a canoe. A 13.5-mile canoe trip will bring you through a buttonwood and white mangrove forest, a salt marsh and offer a look at several of the state's endangered and threatened species. These include wood storks, bald eagles, red cockaded woodpeckers, crocodiles, manatees, Florida black bears, Florida panthers and

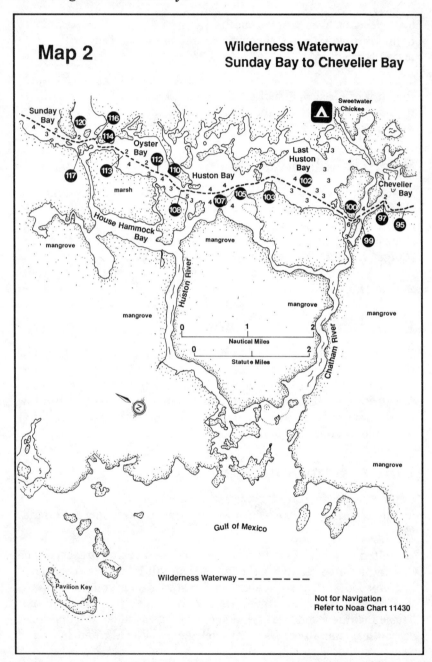

Map 2

**Wilderness Waterway
Sunday Bay to Chevelier Bay**

Sunday
Bay

Oyster
Bay

Huston Bay

Last
Huston
Bay

Chevelier
Bay

marsh

House Hammock Bay

mangrove

Huston River

Chatham River

Sweetwater
Chickee

mangrove

mangrove

mangrove

mangrove

mangrove

0   1   2
Nautical Miles

0   1   2
Statute Miles

N

Gulf of Mexico

Pavilion Key

Wilderness Waterway — — — — —

Not for Navigation
Refer to Noaa Chart 11430

mangrove fox squirrels. Tent and RV camping. Saltwater fishing. Canoe rentals available. Write Collier Seminole State Park, Rt. 4, Box 848, Naples, FL 33961. Phone: 813-394-3397.

FLAMINGO AREA CANOE TRAILS

Nine Mile Pond. This scenic trail starts at the Nine Mile Pond parking lot. It is a loop trail, 5.2 miles in length; travel time is approximately four hours. The trail is marked with white plastic posts. It crosses an open pond and travels through fresh water prairie, sawgrass and mangrove habitat. Watch for alligators, wading birds and an occasional snail kite. The trail may be difficult to follow, but during summer months it is the preferable trail as it is relatively insect-free. During the winter dry season, portions may be impassable due to low water levels. No motors permitted.

Noble Hammock. The trail begins between Nine Mile Pond and the Hell's Bay trail head on the east side of the main park road. The trail passes through open country and small alligator ponds, through buttonwood, red mangrove and sawgrass. Sharp corners and a narrow trail require good maneuvering skills. Historically, the trail was used for access into some of the larger hammocks for bootlegging operations and many of the old cuttings to mark the trail can still be seen. Travel time on the three-mile loop trail, which terminates at the main park road approximately 75 yards south of the trail head, is three hours. Check for low water levels during the dry season. No motors permitted.

Hell's Bay. The trail head is located approximately half-way between Nine Mile Pond and West Lake on the west side of the main park road. A Backcountry Use Permit is recommended when traveling this trail, even when not camping. The bay was supposedly named by old timers because it is "Hell to get into and Hell to get out of." This sheltered route weaves through mangrove lined creeks and ponds to a series of small bays beyond the Lard Can campsite. The trail may be difficult to follow—keep an eye out for markers. The first campsite is approximately four miles from the starting point or three hours travel time. The second campsite is in Hell's Bay and is four miles from the first site, or 4.5 hours

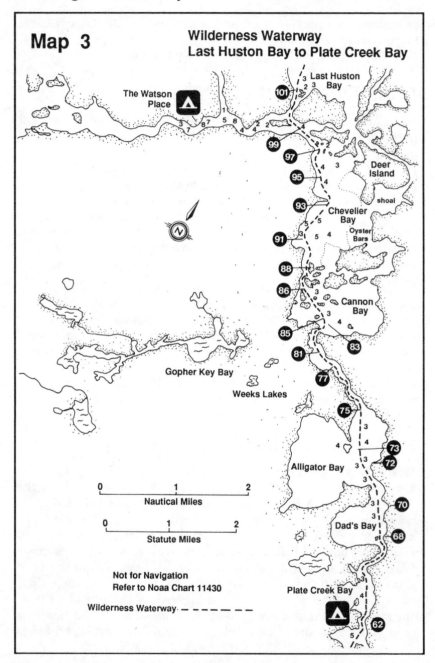

Map 3

Wilderness Waterway
Last Huston Bay to Plate Creek Bay

Last Huston Bay

The Watson Place

Deer Island

shoal

Chevelier Bay

Oyster Bars

Cannon Bay

Gopher Key Bay

Weeks Lakes

Alligator Bay

Dad's Bay

0   1   2
Nautical Miles

0   1   2
Statute Miles

Not for Navigation
Refer to Noaa Chart 11430

Wilderness Waterway – – – – – – –

Plate Creek Bay

travel time. This trail gives the best opportunity to travel through overgrown passageways of red mangrove and brackish water environment. Check the water levels before starting the journey. Use of motors is prohibited from trail head to the Lard Can campsite, but a 5.5 hp motor may be used elsewhere on the trail.

West Lake. This is an eight-mile tour requiring at least seven hours travel time. The trail begins at the West Lake interpretive shelter. You paddle through a series of large open lakes connected by narrow creeks lined with mangroves. Alligators are numerous. This is also a habitat for crocodiles. A long, exposed crossing of West Lake is necessary; use caution on windy days. The trail winds through coastal lake country bordered by red and black mangrove and buttonwood trees and through the remains of a once-great living forest destroyed by hurricanes.

Redfish and sea trout are abundant in the lakes. A small clearing for primitive camping is located at Alligator Creek. 5.5 hp motor maximum—prohibited from the east end of West Lake to Garfield Bight.

Buttonwood Canal is a three-mile trail leading to Coot Bay. Watch for occasional alligators, crocodiles and birds. Give power boats the right of way.

Mud Lake Loop. Enjoy a variety of habitats and wildlife on this loop connecting the Buttonwood Canal, Coot Bay, Mud Lake and along the Bear Lake Canoe Trail. Motors are prohibited. The loop is 4.8 miles starting from the Bear Lake Trail head. It is accessible from the Flamingo Marina through Buttonwood Canal or the Bear Lake Trail head.

Bear Lake Canal. This 11.5-mile route leads to Cape Sable Camping Area, one of the last wilderness beaches left in south Florida. You travel along a narrow, tree-covered historic canal. Accessible from the Flamingo Marina through Buttonwood Canal with a portage or from the Bear Lake Trail head. Impassable between markers 13-17 during the dry season (January through April). Motors prohibited.

Consult NOAA nautical chart 11433 for the location of shoal water (sand bars, mud banks, shallows).

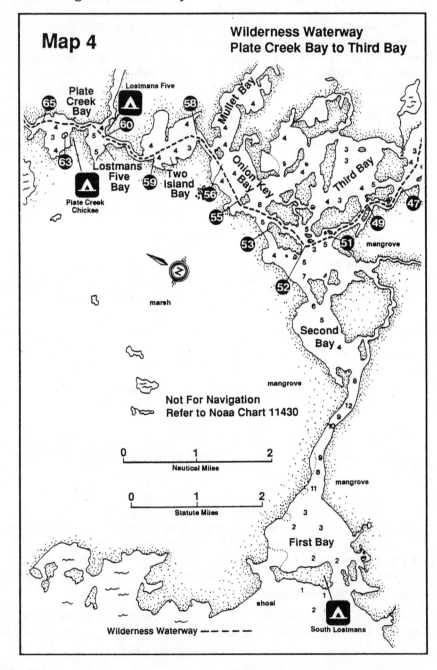

Everglades alligator

Bahia Honda Bridge

Tides can create strong currents. Low tides at East Cape are at least two hours earlier than Flamingo low tides; high tides at East Cape are 1.5 hours earlier than Flamingo high tides.

SAFETY EQUIPMENT CHECKLIST

___ Flotation Gear. Florida law requires a Coast Guard approved personal flotation device for each occupant.

___ First Aid Kit. Add insect repellent and sunscreen.

___ Extra paddle.

___ Bow and stern lines.

___ Flashlight and extra batteries.

___ Compass.

___ Charts.

For additional information write Tropical Everglades Visitor Association, 160 U.S. Highway 1, Florida City FL 33034; phone 305-245-9180.

EVERGLADES CANOE RENTALS

Flamingo Lodge Marina & Outpost Resort
P.O. Box 428
Flamingo FL 33030
305-253-2241 or 813-695-3101

Biscayne Aqua-Center, Inc
P.O. Box 1270
Homestead FL 33030
305-247-2400

Everglades National Park Boat Tours
P.O. Box 119
Everglades City FL 33929
813-695-2591

Kayak, Key Largo

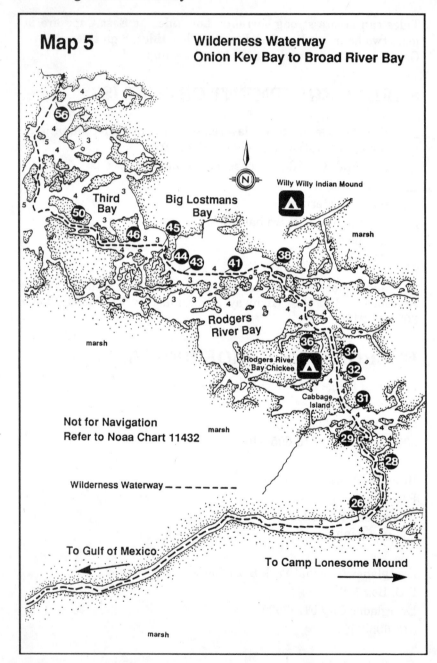

Map 5

**Wilderness Waterway
Onion Key Bay to Broad River Bay**

Third Bay

Big Lostmans Bay

Willy Willy Indian Mound

marsh

Rodgers River Bay

Rodgers River Bay Chickee

Cabbage Island

marsh

**Not for Navigation
Refer to Noaa Chart 11432**

Wilderness Waterway — — — — — —

To Gulf of Mexico

To Camp Lonesome Mound

marsh

CANOE OUTFITTERS

Canoe outfitters offer all-inclusive guided trips, which may include pick-up from the airport, transportation between sites, tents, canoes, and meals. All you are required to bring is yourself and a change of clothing. Rates start at $100 per day. Groups are usually small, 10-12 people. Singles and couples mix. You can bring your own group or join one formed by the outfitter. You must book in advance.

Mountain Workshop, Inc. of Ridgefield CT offers full blown adventure-travel expeditions through Everglades National Park and Florida's Keys including canoeing, airboating, diving, snorkeling, parasailing, hiking and more. Special nature education programs are available for school groups, youngsters (11 -15) and biology study groups. Tours are from November through April (listing below).

Hawk, I'm Your Sister, of Santa Fe, New Mexico offers one annual Everglades canoe tour for women only and one for couples of any configuration.

North American Canoe Tours offers guided and "you-paddle" tours which can be a half-day to a week or longer. They provide everything you need: a 17-foot all-aluminum Grumman canoe, personal flotation devices, paddles for two, a photocopy of local maps, a cooler with ice and drinking water. They also run a low-cost, 10-room bed and breakfast inn, The Ivey House, at Everglades City (listing below).

Wilderness Southeast, a non-profit educational organization, has two Everglades tours. One week-long rugged paddle/hike trip first exploring the terrestrial and freshwater habitats of the northern Everglades, then by canoe or sea kayak, exploring wild beaches, isolated coastal islands and mangrove estuaries of the Ten Thousand Islands area. Primitive camping. A less rugged houseboat/canoe tour originates at the Flamingo Lodge   in Everglades National Park.   Addresses and additional outfitters offering similar expeditions follow:

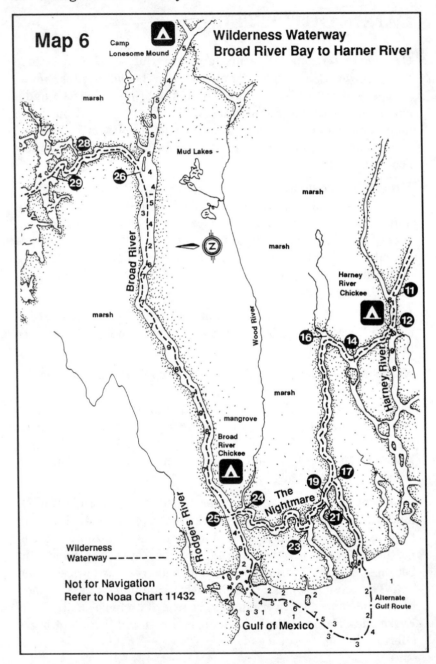

Map 6

Camp
Lonesome Mound

Wilderness Waterway
Broad River Bay to Harner River

marsh

Mud Lakes -

marsh

marsh

Harney
River
Chickee

Broad River

marsh

Wood River

mangrove

Broad
River
Chickee

marsh

Rodgers River

The
Nightmare

Harney River

Wilderness
Waterway -------

Not for Navigation
Refer to Noaa Chart 11432

Alternate
Gulf Route

Gulf of Mexico

Canoe Outpost of Arcadia
Jon Bragg
Rt. 7, Box 301
Arcadia FL 33821
813-494-1215

St. Regis Canoe Outfitters
David Cilley
P.O. Box 318
Lake Clear NY 12945
518-891-1838

The Pike School, Inc.
J. Wolter
P.O. Box 101
Haverhill NH 03765

Women in the Wilderness
J. Niemi
566 Ottawa Ave.
St. Paul MN 55107
612-227-2284

North American Canoe Tours
D. Harraden
(Winter address)
P.O. Box 5038
Everglades City FL 33929
813-695-4666

(Summer address)
65 Black Pt. Rd.
Niantic CT 06357
203-739-0791

Buckley's Mountainside Canoes
4700 West Remus Road
Mt. Pleasant MI 48858
517-772-5437

Mountain Workshop, Inc.
Corky Clark
P.O. Box 625
Ridgefield CT 06877
203-438-3640

Wild Rivers
Gray Smith
20 Coolidge Ave.
White Plains NY 10606
914-949-5282

Wilderness Southeast
711 Sandtown Road
Savannah GA 31410
914-897-5108

Hawk I'm Your Sister
Beverly Antaeus
P.O. Box 9109
Santa Fe NM 87504
505-984-2268

Uncommon Adventures
Michael Gray
P.O. Box 6065
East Lansing MI 48823
517-641-6987

Ibis Tours
Bardy Jones
1000 South Federal Highway
Boynton Beach FL 33435
407-738-5512 or 6100

ROWING EXPEDITIONS

If you like rowing rather than canoe or kayak paddling, Tortugas Rowing Expeditions offers very rugged expeditions dedicated to fitness, education, environmental study, and group cooperation. Captain John Duke takes you to wondrous beaches aboard 32-foot-long boats which are similar to the old whale boats. They are built of marine plywood, and fiberglassed over. There are rowing stations for six rowers and one helmsperson. Each rower uses an oar 12 to 14 feet long. The craft are seaworthy and capable of withstanding rough sea conditions. Tortugas tours are for those of you in excellent condition who want to be challenged, both mentally and physically. Write to Tortugas Rowing Expeditions, Rt. 4, Box 902, Summerland Key FL 33042; phone 305-872-3536.

ADDITIONAL READING

Two good booklets on canoeing in the Everglades are "Boat and Canoe Camping-Everglades Backcountry & Ten Thousand Islands Region" ($3.95, 64 pp. paper) and "Guide to the Wilderness Waterway of the Everglades National Park" ($9.95, 64 pp. paper). Add $2 per book for shipping.

Available from Florida National Parks & Monuments Association, Inc.
P.O. Box 279, Homestead FL 33030

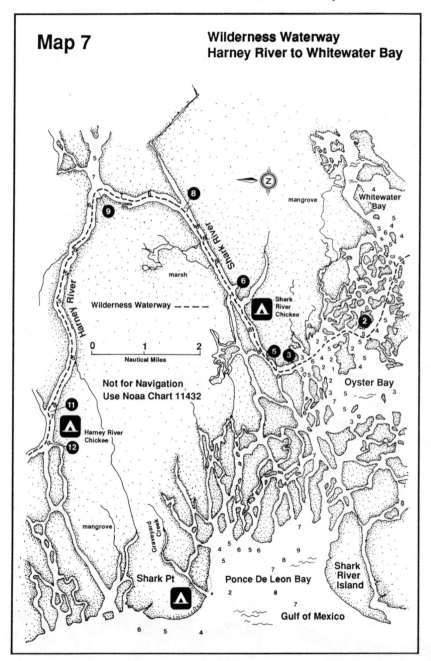

Map 7

Wilderness Waterway
Harney River to Whitewater Bay

Whitewater Bay

mangrove

Shark River

Z

8

9

marsh

6

Wilderness Waterway — — —

Shark
River
Chickee

2

0   1   2

Nautical Miles

5   3

Oyster Bay

Not for Navigation
Use Noaa Chart 11432

Harney River

11

Harney River
Chickee

12

mangrove

Graveyard Creek

Shark Pt

Ponce De Leon Bay

Shark
River
Island

Gulf of Mexico

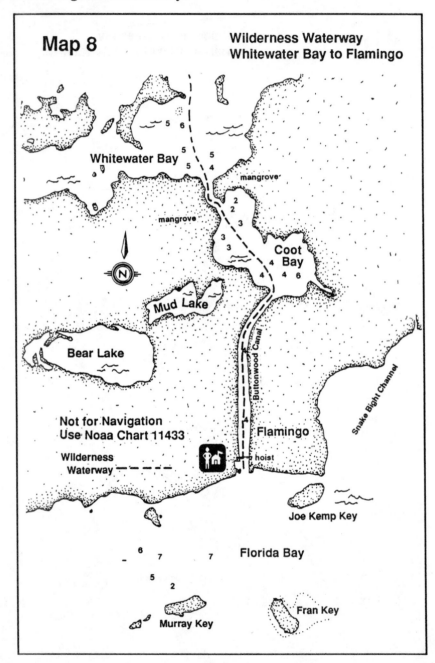

Map 8

Wilderness Waterway
Whitewater Bay to Flamingo

5 6

Whitewater Bay

5   5
5   4

mangrove

2
2

mangrove   3

3

3   Coot
Bay

4

4   4 6

Mud Lake

Bear Lake

Not for Navigation
Use Noaa Chart 11433

Wilderness
Waterway

Buttonwood Canal

4   Flamingo

hoist

Snake Bight Channel

Joe Kemp Key

Florida Bay

6   7   7

5
2

Fran Key

Murray Key

CYCLING TRAILS

Whether you want to explore for a day or a season, self-guided cycling tours are one of the best ways to discover the Everglades and the Florida Keys.

Flat terrain and well marked trails lead you over miles of scenic bridges, through wildlife preserves, exotic bird sanctuaries, palm-lined beaches, and historic parks. Watersport opportunities are endless. A wide range of accommodations exist throughout the area including picturesque, oceanside campgrounds.

If historic Key West is your destination, you'll find cycling ideal for touring the southernmost city. Bike rentals and services are widely available. Racks where you may stand or lock your bike are everywhere.

Traffic along U.S. 1, the main highway through the Keys, once posed a serious danger to road riders. Today's cyclists find wider shoulders on the bridges and a well-marked bike trail for most of the 106-mile route between Key Largo and Key West.

The main road and bicycling trails through Everglades National Park are well maintained.

PLANNING YOUR TOUR

Visit Everglades National Park from December through March. The rest of the year brings torrential downpours and thick clouds of mosquitos.

The best time to tour Florida's Keys is from December through

May. Skies are predictably sunny and air temperatures range from 75 to 85° F.

Equipment

Single-speed, coaster-brake bikes are as at home in south Florida as are hi-tech, 21-speed mountain bikes. Most of the land is flat and low-lying, usually just a few feet above sea level. The most uphill pedaling you'll encounter is over bridges. Rental bikes are all single-speed with baskets.

Wide tires are best for the gravel and dirt trails that are intermittent with paved sections.

For short rides in the populated areas tools and spare equipment are usually not necessary. If you plan long distance road riding, carry equipment sufficient to repair and inflate a tire, a spare inner-tube, some cash, sunblock, a first aid kit, bug repellent and fluid container.

Clothing and Gear

Clothing should be loose and lightweight. Cotton or Spandex cycling shorts and loose shirts are the best choice. The new mesh cycling fabrics, available at most bike shops, wick perspiration away from your body and keep you cool. Chafing and skin irritation in the groin area can be reduced by use of a sheepskin seat cover, available in most of the bike rental shops.

The climate, relaxed atmosphere and fact that the bike trails and old bridges are free of automobile traffic sway many cyclists into wearing baseball caps or straw hats instead of safety helmets. Nowadays, this is an unnecessary risk. There are many new helmets, designed for tropical wear, that will keep you cool and protect your head and face. Insure a proper fit by shopping for one before your trip. To prevent serious injury in a fall or crash, avoid pushing the helmet back onto the top of your head.

For mid-winter travel pack a windbreaker. An occasional cold front during the winter months has dropped temperatures as low as 40° F, though 75° F is more usual.

Dehydration and Heat Stroke

In summer and fall when midday temperatures soar beyond the comfort zone for riding, consider other activities. Plan cycling time for cooler morning or evening hours.

If you are not acclimated to hot weather riding, limit your tours to short distances and slow speeds. Avoid wearing long-sleeve jerseys and long tights, and drink plenty of cold fluid-replacement beverages to avoid heat stroke or dehydration.

Insulated fluid pouches such as ThermalBak or IceBak will keep fluids cool for several hours. For very short tours an insulated drink holder that clips on the handlebars may be purchased at most of the area bike shops.

Symptoms of heat exhaustion or heat stroke are weakness, headache, nausea and fainting. For treatment seek immediate medical aid. If the person is conscious, give cold fluids and continuously wet down the skin with moist towels while enroute to a hospital.

Transporting Your Bicycle

Most airlines, bus companies and Amtrak will supply a special bicycle box which enables you to carry your bike as baggage. This, in theory, insures the bike arriving intact when you do. The box cost runs $12-$18. For transport, the handlebars, front wheel and pedals are removed.

You can have your bike shop box it for you before your trip. Be sure they use bubble pack or foam to protect it. Get a clear demonstration on how to put it back together.

Check to see if your airline(s) has a pressurized baggage compartment. If not, you must deflate the tires. Unpressurized compartments will cause the tires to swell and possibly burst. This may result in rim damage.   (All major U.S. carriers have pressurized baggage compartments.)

Be sure to make a reservation for your bicycle. During high travel times—holidays or peak season—when the baggage compartment is loaded with standard luggage you may be forced to ship your bike as freight.

CYCLING EVERGLADES NATIONAL PARK

The main park entrance is 45 miles from Miami International Airport. There are no regularly scheduled bus tours or public transportation to or within the park, but Greyhound Bus Company will take you along U.S. 1 to Route 9336, Florida City which is 11 miles from the main park entrance. From there you can cycle Route 9336—a paved road through a residential and farm area. Signs on the highway will point you in the proper direction—a right turnoff from the southbound lane onto 9336. Greyhound buses leave three times daily from the airport-vicinity bus station located at 4111 N.W. 27 Street, Miami FL 33142 (305-876-7123) and the Homestead terminal at 5 N.E. 3rd Road, Homestead FL 33030 (305-247-2040).

Avoid cycling the entire distance from the airport. There is no shoulder, and traffic is fast-moving and heavy. Transporting your bike by bus or car is a safer choice.

There is an entrance fee that is good for seven days: $5 per private motorized vehicle or $2 per person entering by bicycle. At the Main Visitor Center, open daily from 8 am till 5 pm, you can view a 15-minute introductory film, displays and pick up schedules of park activities. Books, postcards, insect repellent and other items are sold here.

The main park road begins at the visitor center, wanders through the Pinelands and ends 38 miles later at Flamingo. The road is paved and well-maintained. Several cycling trails take off from this road and a few more begin at Flamingo. Horseback riders occasionally use these trails—use caution and quietly give them the right-of-way when passing.

The north end of the park can be best explored along Shark Valley Loop.

If transporting your bike to the Everglades by car, you may park at the Royal Palm Visitor Center parking lot, Long Pine Key picnic area or Flamingo Outpost. If you plan to camp you will need a backcountry permit, available free at the Main Visitor Center.

The only overnight visitor accommodations within the park are at Flamingo Lodge, located 38 miles southwest of the Main Visitor Center.

Camping is on a first-come, first-served basis. Flamingo has 60 tent sites and 235 drive-in sites. Long Pine Key has 108 sites. During the winter, campgrounds fill every night. Plan to arrive early in the day.

Modern comfort stations and drinking water are available at both sites; cold-water showers at Flamingo only. Limited groceries and camping supplies may be purchased at the Flamingo Marina Store.

Swimming in the park is discouraged. Fresh water ponds have alligators; salt water areas are shallow with mucky bottoms. Underwater visibility is extremely poor and sharks and barracudas abound.

Everglades National Park Cycling Trails

SHARK VALLEY LOOP

Shark Valley Loop, a 15-mile road that circuits the northern portion of Everglades National Park, lies off U.S 41, the Tamiami Trail, 50 miles from the Main Visitor Center. This road edges a wide shallow waterway crowded with dense fields of sawgrass—the headwaters for Shark River. Alligators, otters, deer, raccoons, frogs, snakes, turtles and birds, including rare wood storks and snail kites, inhabit this watery expanse. Hardwood hammocks and other tree islands dot the landscape. The loop road, originally constructed by oil prospectors, is used for tram rides, bicycles and walking. A 65-ft observation tower along the road provides a spectacular bird's-eye view.

For your safety use extreme caution when stopping for trams. The shoulder is very steep. Be sure to come to a complete stop before dismounting and pulling to the side of the road. Watch out for snakes and alligators. Venomous pygmy rattlesnakes are common on high ground during the wet season. Also avoid touching poison ivy, poisonwood trees or the sawgrass which can inflict nasty cuts.

Bicycles may be rented next to the ticket booth daily from 8:30 am to 3pm. Cycling along the Tamiami Trail is not recommended—traffic is fast moving, services are few and the road shoulder is soft.

THE PINELANDS

A network of interconnecting trails runs through the Pinelands, an unusually diverse pine forest. Under the pine canopy are about 200 types of plants, including 30 found nowhere else on Earth. Whitetail deer, opossums, raccoons and the endangered Florida panther live in the Pinelands. You can also see turtles, lizards and snakes, exotic zebra butterflies, striped grasshoppers, red-bellied woodpeckers, orchids and tree snails.

The bicycle trails, a series of one-lane fire roads, are well maintained. Avoid those marked for hiking only; they may be mucky and impassable by bike.

MAHOGANY TRAIL

The turn off for Mahogany Hammock Trail is about 20 miles from the Main Visitor Center. The distance from the main road is about two miles. No facilities.

Mahogany is a walking trail, but one of the favorites in the park and worth making a side trip to see. You can leave your bicycle in the parking lot. The trail is a raised boardwalk, first over swamp then into a dense jungle-like environment. In contrast to the surrounding marshlands, here you can view red-headed woodpeckers and orchids growing in the tree tops, rare paurotis palms and towering mahogany trees, including the largest living specimen in the United States. Huge golden orb spider webs are suspended from the tree branches; colorful liguus tree snails inhabit the bark. At night, barred owls awaken to hunt.

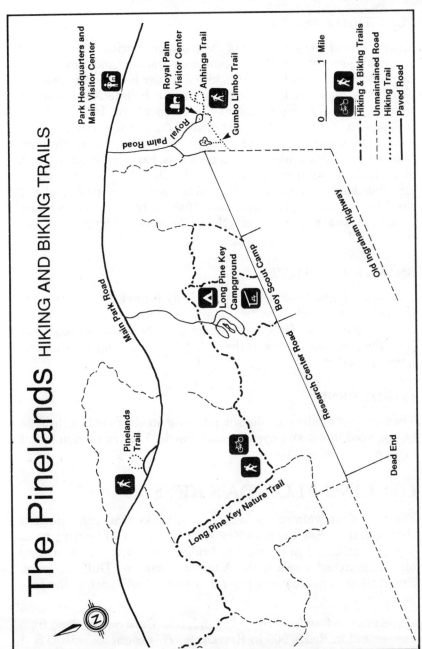

The Pinelands HIKING AND BIKING TRAILS

Park Headquarters and Main Visitor Center

Royal Palm Visitor Center

Anhinga Trail

Royal Palm Road

Gumbo Limbo Trail

Main Park Road

Long Pine Key Campground

Boy Scout Camp

Old Ingraham Highway

Research Center Road

Pinelands Trail

Long Pine Key Nature Trail

Dead End

0   1   Mile

Hiking & Biking Trails
Unmaintained Road
Hiking Trail
Paved Road

FLAMINGO AREA TRAILS

Flamingo is at the south end of the park, on Florida Bay. It is the principal jump-off point for canoeing, fishing and boating in Everglades National Park. It is also a leader in mosquito production. Bug repellent is needed year round. In late November we were fogged in by mosquitos at the campground, but found the trails north of Flamingo and the paved area at the marina less inhabited by these pests. The camp store (open mid-Nov. through mid-March) rents canoes, stocks groceries, camping supplies, bait and fuel. Flamingo Marina and Outpost Resort offers air-conditioned rooms, spacious cabins, camping, a pool, and gift shop. It also offers wilderness tours, fishing trips and tram tours. In season, you can rent a bicycle at the shack outside the camp store.

SNAKE BIGHT TRAIL

This is a rugged 1.6-mile, one-way shady tunnel through tropical hardwood hammock. The trail starts six miles east of Flamingo from the park road. Good bird watching exists in the wooded areas from the short boardwalk at the end of the trail. Alligators are frequently spotted.

ROWDY BEND

The trail is 2.6 miles. Cyclists wind along an old road bed through buttonwood forest and open coastal prairie. The trail is somewhat overgrown with grasses.

CYCLING FLORIDA'S KEYS

Florida's Keys welcome cyclists. A paved bike trail runs much of the route from Key Largo to Key West. It breaks off in some spots and crosses U.S. 1 in places. The bridges have wide shoulders and offer unmatched views of the Atlantic Ocean and Gulf-side bays. Fragrant, orange-flowered poinciana trees shade part of the bike path.

If you are starting from the mainland, take Card Sound Road from Homestead to Route 905 in Key Largo. This connects with U.S. 1

and bypasses almost 30 miles of it. About 15 miles into Key Largo you pick up a paved bike trail on the ocean side of the highway. Greyhound will transport you and your boxed bike to any point along U.S. 1 from the airport-vicinity terminal.

Finding your way around is easy; mile markers (green signs with white numbers) are posted each mile along U.S. 1 throughout Florida's Keys. They start with 126, just south of Florida City and end with the zero marker at the corner of Fleming and Whitehead streets in Key West.

KEY LARGO AND THE UPPER KEYS

Key Largo is often the focus of a Florida Keys vacation. The bike trail begins at mile marker 106. Heading south you'll pass a long stretch of trailers and billboards offering diving, snorkeling and fishing. All along U.S. 1 you can rent boats, jet skis or stop to relax at waterfront resorts or restaurants. Dive shops are everywhere. At the Italian Fisherman, a large marina, restaurant and beach complex at MM 104, you can take a swim in the bay or the pool, rent a windsurfer, Hobie Cat sailboat or jet ski.

A left turn at MM 103.2 will bring you to the Key Largo Undersea Park. This is the sight of the first underwater hotel, Jules' Undersea Lodge. For $12 you can snorkel the lagoon, though a better choice for a snorkeling tour would be an ocean reef trip. There is usually one available each morning and afternoon from John Pennekamp Coral Reef State Park. To enter the park turn left at the sign at MM 102.5. The park offers oceanside camping, picnic areas, showers, rest rooms, bike racks, a dive shop, reef trips, snack bar, aquarium, and gift shop. It has two protected swimming beaches; sailboat, powerboat and canoe rentals; glass bottom boat rides and a nature walk. Reservations for camping at John Pennekamp should be made in advance. For information, write to John Pennekamp Coral Reef State Park, P.O. Box 487, Key Largo FL 33037 or phone 305-451-1202.

At MM 102 you'll pass The Quay on the bay side of the highway. The Quay is a casual beach club open to everyone. It has beautiful palm-lined grounds, a formal indoor/outdoor restaurant and an informal beach-side mesquite grill, a bayside pool, a small beach and

The Florida Keys

Biscayne

FLORIDA BAY

Gulf of Mexico

Key Largo

Tavernier

Islamorada

Sugarloaf Key

Big Pine Key

Marathon

Long Key

Stock Island

Grassy Key

Atlantic Ocean

Seven Mile Bridge

Boca Chica

Bahia Honda

Key West

70 miles to Fort Jefferson

0   10   20
Miles

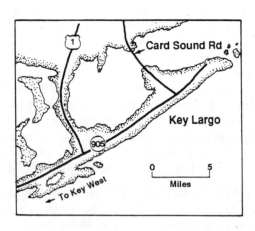

1

Card Sound Rd

Key Largo

905

To Key West

0   5
Miles

a relaxing atmosphere. Sunset cruises leave from the Quay dock.

Continuing south, the bike path leads to the Holiday Inn docks at MM 100. Here you can view the *African Queen*, made famous by Humphrey Bogart and Katherine Hepburn in the 1951 film classic.

At MM 99.5, just past the shopping center, the highway splits around a median. After passing the traffic light, keep to the left on the southbound side. Here you'll find Key Largo Bikes which offers sales, service, repairs, rentals and supplies. Phone: 305-451-1910.

Key Largo ends at the Tavernier Creek Bridge, MM 91. The bike path stops, but you can ride on the old highway to your left. Be careful. Automobiles use this as a secondary road. On the bay side is the Tavernier Creek Marina, where you'll find a snack bar, dive shop and boat rentals.

A left turn onto Burton Drive at MM 92.6 leads to Harry Harris County Park, a good spot for a swim and a picnic. The park opens at 8 am.

The Snake Creek Bridge, MM 87, crosses to Windley Key and Islamorada where you can sign up for a snorkel trip to explore the sunken Spanish ship, *Herrara*, or arrange to swim with dolphins or pet a shark at Theatre of the Sea (MM 85.5). Plan a stop at the Holiday Isle beach complex, MM 84. There is a white sand beach, tropical pools, rooftop and beach-side restaurants, and nightly entertainment. You can sail, sunbathe, snorkel, fish, scuba, jetski, windsurf, parasail, swim or rent an inflatable island and drift off to sea.

At MM 78.5, a 24-passenger boat leaves for Indian Key, a historic preserve and Lignumvitae Key, a state botanical site. From Islamorada (also known as Upper Matecumbe Key) ride south over Teatable Bridge and Indian Key Bridge to Lower Matecumbe Key.

On Fiesta Key (MM 70) is a KOA Campground with Tent and RV sites, a game room, laundry, two Jacuzzis, and a camp store. There are motels and resorts nearby too.

For oceanside tent camping, continue another mile and a half to Long Key State Park at MM 67.5. The park opens at 8 am and closes at sunset year-round. Here you can swim or fish in the Atlantic and enjoy a hike on the nature trail.

The bike trail outside the park is well maintained, but watch for fast growing tree roots that occasionally surface through the pavement.

THE MIDDLE KEYS

The Marathon area begins the Middle Keys—from Conch Key (MM 62.5) to the Seven Mile Bridge (MM 47).

Leaving Long Key Park toward Key West, you cross a 2.5-mile bridge to Conch Key and Grassy Key. Ocean and bay views from this bridge are splendid. Just beyond the bridge on Duck Key (MM 61) is Hawk's Cay Marina, an oasis offering glass bottom boat tours, boat rentals, diving, snorkeling and fishing charters. The sprawling marina/resort has 177 spacious rooms, a sandy beach, swimming lagoon and four restaurants. There are bike rentals for day trippers.

Next comes Grassy Key, MM 59, home base to the Dolphin Research Center which offers unique educational programs including backcountry field trips, and swimming with dolphins.

For the next few miles the path winds alongside mangrove swamps that edge the highway. Be sure to stock up on cold beverages as there are few commercial establishments until you reach the Days Inn & Marina at MM 54 where you will find suntan lotion, postcards and stamps for sale at Trader Ric's Tropical Apparel and Provisions. Bike rentals too.

See Paul at the KCB Bike Shop (MM 53) for supplies, parts or repairs. KCB rents beach cruiser bikes and kid's bikes. Phone: 305-289-1670.

At MM 52 the bike path passes Marathon airport and the City of Marathon, a bustling resort community with sportfishing as the main attraction. There are several restaurants and motel accommodations. A two-mile ride down Sombrero Beach Road at MM 50, ocean side, will bring you to Sombrero Beach Park. Here you'll find picnic areas, rest rooms and a swimming beach.

As you continue toward Key West the sea turns a prettier shade of turquoise and the scenery get better; the smell of salt in the air grows stronger. Seagulls and pelicans perch on the bridge railings. Sweeping ocean panoramas offer dramatic photo opportunities.

LOWER KEYS

MM 47 begins the Seven Mile Bridge and the Lower Keys, a natural wilderness area. If you are touring locally and don't wish to cross all seven miles of bridge, travel along the adjacent old bridge. Auto traffic is not permitted and you'll usually find other cyclists, especially on a weekend. If you are travelling to the lower Keys and Key West, the old bridge won't get you there. It stops after a few miles. Instead travel along the shoulder of the new automobile bridge. The bike trail area before the bridge is patchy with gravel and grass. It becomes a grassy shoulder after the bridge, more level on the bayside.

The first patch of land after crossing the Seven Mile Bridge is Little Duck Key (MM 40). On the ocean side is a lovely, small sand beach with shaded picnic tables. This is a good spot to peel off some clothing and take a swim.

Two more bridges pass over Missouri Key and Sunshine Key (formerly Ohio Key), a 75-acre camping island at MM 39. The sprawling campground features 400 sites, a marina, grocery store, tennis courts, pool, and every other imaginable amenity. Write to Sunshine Key Camping Resort, Box 790, Sunshine Key FL 33040. Phone: 305-872-2217.

At MM 38, the trail enters Bahia Honda State Park. Named for its "deep bay" by the Spanish, the park is one of the prettiest in the Keys. It caters to 200,000 day visitors per year. Swimming sites are on the Atlantic and Gulf sides; both beaches have sandy bottoms. It also has bay- and ocean-side camp sites, a nature trail, marina and dive shop.

There are three furnished duplex cabins (six units) in the park that accommodate eight people each. Linens and utensils are provided. Snacks and limited grocery items are available at the concession building. Shaded picnic tables are at the old bridge.

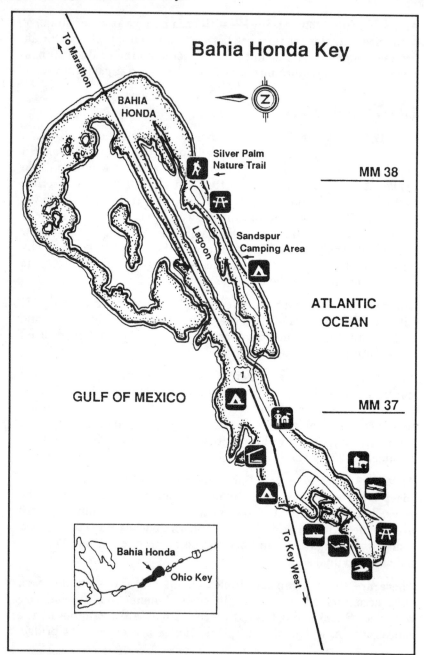

Bahia Honda Key

To Marathon

BAHIA HONDA

Silver Palm Nature Trail

MM 38

Lagoon

Sandspur Camping Area

ATLANTIC OCEAN

GULF OF MEXICO

1

MM 37

To Key West

Bahia Honda

Ohio Key

The park opens at 8 am and closes at sunset. For further information write, Bahia Honda State Recreation Area, Box 782, Big Pine Key FL 33043; phone 305-872-2353.

The Bahia Honda Bridge crosses to Summerland Key (MM 35), a jumping off point to explore offshore Looe Key Marine Sanctuary.

MM 33 begins Big Pine Key, a pine forest island complete with free-roaming, miniature Key deer. A right turn on Key Deer Boulevard (MM 30.5) will bring you to the refuge area for the deer. This area is also a refuge for the great white heron. After you make the turn off from U.S. 1, stay on the south side of the street where green striping marks the bike trail.

Refuge headquarters are about two miles off to the left on Watson Boulevard. If you ride another mile and a half down Key Deer Boulevard and turn left onto Big Pine Street the path cuts into thick stands of pine and palm trees toward the Blue Hole where several large alligators make their home.

You may have trouble spotting the tiny, two-ft Key deer. They come out only during dusk and early morning. Feeding is prohibited. It lures them into the roadway where many have been struck by cars.

Watch out for huge webs of the golden orb spiders in the hardwood forest.

There are 25 miles of low, wet ground, mangroves and RV parks between Big Pine Key and Key West. The bike path is intermittent with grassy or gravel shoulders. The incline in a few spots will force you to ride on the highway for a bit. Keep to the side as much as possible. You can see coral patches and distant mangrove islands from the bridges and there are spots to stop and take a swim. Avoid exploring dirt roads leading into back woods.

At MM 28.5, Parmer's Place (305-872-2157) rents comfortable, waterfront cottages.

Sugarloaf Key, MM 20, has a resort with a dolphin show, boat ramp and comfortable air-conditioned rooms. At MM 17, behind the Sugarloaf Lodge, is a vacant bat tower, a reminder of a failed attempt to lure the mosquito-hungry creatures into the area.

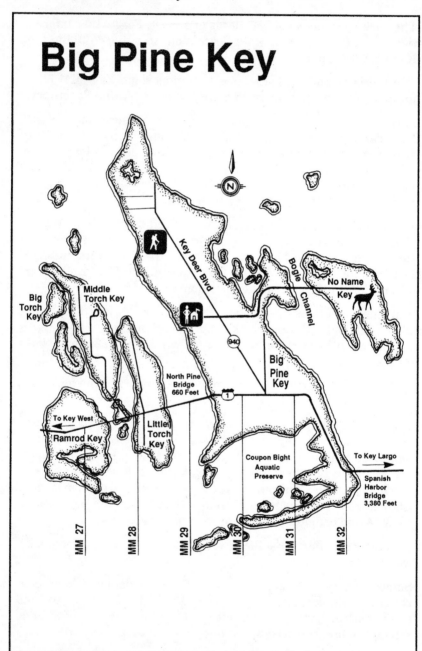

Big Pine Key

Just past the Saddlebunch Keys, the bike path picks up on the bay side.

Big Coppitt Key (MM 11-MM 7), is home base to the Key West Naval Air Station at Boca Chica, where thundering F-16s slice the sky above. Nearer to earth, low-flying ospreys stand quiet guard over their pole-top nests.

Another mile brings you to Stock Island, your final approach to Key West. Named for cows and pigs kept here in early days, the island is partially a service area for municipal offices and the site of the community dump.

A right turn onto Junior College Road, just before the Key West Bridge, will bring you to the Key West Seaplane Base where you can charter a half-day snorkeling excursion to Fort Jefferson. The Key West Resort Golf Course, Tennessee Williams Fine Arts Center, and Florida Keys Hospital share the island.

Key West

After crossing the bridge into Key West go right or left on the paved bike trail that skirts the shore line on both North and South Roosevelt Boulevards. Either route will lead you to the historic heart of Florida's Keys, Old Town Key West. If you arrive by car, boat, ship or plane you'll find rental bikes at hotels and in town. Cycling is the favored way to avoid congested traffic and tour the city.

A right turn from the Key West Bridge brings you past a commercial strip of hotels and restaurants, Garrison's Bight and the Key West Yacht Club. Farther on, North Roosevelt turns into Truman Avenue. Truman later intersects Duval Street which leads to the historic section. The bike path ends with North Roosevelt Boulevard, but picks up again on the south side of the island at Higgs Beach.

A right turn on Whitehead Street leads to Mallory Square area and the center of activity. Be sure to obey the one-way street signs as cyclists are ticketed for going the wrong way.

A left turn at the Key West Bridge along South Roosevelt

Boulevard brings you past the airport, the Salt Pond—an ecological preserve, Smathers Beach and Higgs Beach. The bike path stops at the south end of Higgs Beach. A right turn will lead to Truman Avenue.

The area on and around Caroline Street is shaded by huge tropical poinciana and palm trees. Stop by the Chamber of Commerce on Wall Street in the Mallory Square area for a copy of the Solares Hill Walking and Biking Guide that details every inch of the city. Additional bike paths throughout the city are in the planning stages.

KEY WEST BICYCLE RENTALS

Moped Hospital, 601 Truman Ave; phone 296-3344

Bicycle Center, 523 Truman Ave; phone 294-4556

Bubba's Bike Rental, 705 Duval St; phone 294-2618

The Bike Shop, 1110 Truman Ave; phone 294-1073

Higgs Beach, Key West

FISHING

A day of fishing anywhere is great, but in the Everglades and Florida Keys, it's better! Where else can you catch bonefish from a dock, a tarpon or permit from a bridge, a marlin from a charter boat and even sea trout in a backyard canal? Here's a run down on what to expect offshore, back country (mangrove flats—Florida Bay & Ten Thousand Islands region), from a party boat, a head boat, a bridge, and even onshore.

OFFSHORE

Charter boats are just that. You book them for a deep-sea fishing trip and they take care of the rest. Bait, tackle and ice are usually provided, and fish, all kinds of fish from tail dancing sailfish and marlin, or reel-smoking wahoo and colorful, fabulous dolphin (the fish, not Flipper) to delicious yellowtail and mutton snapper, grouper and kingfish, all in their season.

The captains are professional and really aim to please. They will stay out as long as the angler doesn't give up. Key West Captain Bill Wickers' favorite "one that got away" tale is of a 700-lb marlin hooked from his boat, the *Linda D*, at 1:10 pm on 50 lb line. The fish put up a fight for the entire day and was brought to the boat at least 10 or 12 times. The angler held steady long after sunset, certain the fish would tire. At 10:30 p.m. the marlin let go and swam away.

Reproduced, in part, with permission from an article by Bob T. Epstein

The charter boats cater to parties of four to six persons with day rates averaging about $500 for everything except lunch, beverages and suntan lotion. Light tackle boats can accommodate one or two fishermen at substantially lower rates. Party boat tariffs average $20 for full-day trips, including tackle.

In Key West where the ocean meets the Gulf there is always a calm area to fish. On the Gulf side the boats troll for barracuda, kingfish and bonito. Oceanside catches are usually sailfish and dolphin.

ACCOMMODATIONS

A few of the fishing marinas offer accommodations as well as guides and charters. Bud N' Mary's in Islamorada offers motel rooms, a penthouse apartment, and an oceanfront beach house. Hawk's Cay offers luxury resort accommodations.

WHERE TO BOOK A CHARTER

Charter boats are everywhere and may be booked through many resorts and at any large marina. Key West's city marina has 36 charter boats lined up and ready to go.

EVERGLADES TEN THOUSAND ISLANDS AREA

Captain Dave Prickett
Island Charters
Box 172
Chokoloskee FL 33925
813-695-2286

Captain Bob Chipman
P.O. Box 37
Everglades City FL 33929
813-695-2258

NORTH KEY LARGO

J-Ron's Marina
MM 104-2
305-451-4684

Perdue-Dean Inc
Ocean Reef Club
North Key Largo
305-367-2661

Gilbert's Motel & Marina
MM 108
305-451-1133

Key Largo Holiday Harbour Inc
MM 100 Oceanside
305-451-3661

Tavernier Creek Marina
MM 90.5
305-852-5854

ISLAMORADA

Robbies
Holiday Isle Docks
MM 84.5
305-664-8498
305-664-4196

Bud N' Mary's Marina
MM 79.5
305-664-2461

Whale Harbor Dock
U.S. Highway 1
305-664-4511

MARATHON

7 Mile Marina
MM 47.5 (at 7 mile bridge)
305-743-7712

Hawk's Cay Resort and Marina
MM 61
Duck Key
305-743-9000

KEY WEST

Charter Row
Amberjack Pier
North Roosevelt Avenue,
Garrison Bight, Key West

PARTY BOATS OR HEAD BOATS

If you're interested in rubbing elbows with lots of other fishermen,
and want to share a fine fishing and people-watching experience,
try a party boat or head boat. It's an inexpensive way to fish
off-shore. Bait and tackle are provided. You may even make new
friends and catch dinner: snappers, groupers, even dolphin and
sailfish are caught off party boats. Sharks, too! Anyway you go,
even in your own boat or a rental boat, offshore is a must, a real
Keys experience.

Deep Sea Party Boats

KEY LARGO

Captain Jack Fishing Fleet
Holiday Inn Docks, MM 100
305-451-4425

Fantastic Charters Inc
Holiday Inn Docks, MM 100
305-451-2890 or 451-5740

Captain Jackie McGuire
Holiday Inn Docks, MM 100
305-451-4425

Sailor's Choice
Holiday Inn Docks, MM 100
305-451-1802

ISLAMORADA

Robbies
Holiday Isle Docks (South End)
MM 84.5
P.O. Box 86
Islamorada FL 33036
Docks: 305-664-8498/664-8070
Office: 305-664-4196

Gulf Lady Party Fishing Boat
Bud N' Mary's Marina
MM 79.5
Islamorada FL 33036
305-664-2628/664-2461

MARATHON

Marathon Lady Party Boats
Vaca Cut Marathon
305-743-5580

Winner Party Boats
MM 50
(behind Marathon Band)
Winner Sombrero Docks
305-743-6969

KEY WEST

Gulfstream III
City Marina/Amberjack Pier #8
Garrison Bight
305-296-8494

Capt. John's Greyhound V
Amberjack Pier/City Marina
Garrison Bight

BACK COUNTRY FISHING
FLORIDA BAY, TEN THOUSAND ISLANDS REGION

Back country is exactly what it says, out back in the wild beautiful
Florida Bay and Ten Thousand Islands region. White pelicans,
egrets, or cormorants make a beautiful backdrop for fishing these
mostly flat waters. Folks who don't like offshore usually love the
back country. Sea trout, redfish, jacks, tarpon, snook are all just
some of the fish you can catch out there in "God's
Country"—where man's footprints are rare and nature's hand is
heavy!

BRIDGE AND SHORE FISHING

For the casual visitor who has no intention of boating due to time
restrictions, fear of sea sickness, who has little ones or is sunburn
prone, fishing from shore or a bridge is for you. Snapper, grouper,
sheepshead, permit and even tarpon can and are caught from the
Keys bridges. There are more than two dozen bridges that accommodate fishermen and sightseers. You can watch pelicans, egrets,
seagulls and osprey feed and preen their feathers only feet away.
Here, too, the people are friendly and the sights are varied. It can
be really exciting, especially when a fisherman hooks up with the
"silver king", and the tarpon zooms parallel to the bridge.
Everyone moves very quickly, as a hundred pounds or more of
shimmering beauty and strength tests the angler. All who witness
get to see a battle with a sporting giant of the fish clan, the tar-

Airboat, Miccosukee Indian Village

Boardwalk, Corkscrew Swamp Sanctuary, Naples

Key West from the air

Everglades Pelican

pon. Fishing from shore, or wading with lures or bait, you can catch the spectacular bonefish or hook a barracuda. For the neophyte, a toothy and tough 'cuda is fun, but not difficult to entice.

In Everglades City, along Route 29 or the Tamiami Trail you can fish the roadside canals almost anywhere you can find a parking space.

Whatever your fishing pleasure, you won't be disappointed in the Everglades or Florida Keys.

A much-applauded new trend that many Floridian fishermen are practicing is a catch-and-release policy for "trophy-fish" that were previously killed for wall mounting.

"It insures some good fishing for our grandchildren," remarked one charter captain.

Many Keys marinas feature lifelike replicas of favorite gamefish so anglers need no kill to go home with a photo of their catch. The International Gamefish Release and Enhancement Foundation, Inc. is a non-profit organization with the principal goal of encouraging releases. The group's credo says it all: "It takes a good fisherman to catch a fish, but it takes a great fisherman to release it."

FLY FISHING SCHOOL

The Florida Keys Fly Fishing School provides fly fishermen of all skill levels with an opportunity to learn or improve their saltwater fly fishing skills and techniques. The school specializes in catching the tropical flats species such as tarpon, bonefish, snook, permit, redfish and mutton snapper by sight fishing with fly rods on the flats.

Classes are usually held at Plantation Yacht Harbor in Islamorada, Florida Keys. They do not include actual fishing, but cover casting, sighting fish, fly selection, fly tying, fly presentation, tackle specification and selection, leaders, knots, fighting fish, wind problems, flats etiquette, short and quick casting, selecting fly fishing guides and more. Films, slides, and field exer-

Glass bottom boat, Discovery, *Key West*

cises are used to give broad coverage. Students are given plenty of personal attention.

The instructor staff is a "Who's Who" of saltwater fly fishermen, including Stu Apte, author of *Fishing in the Florida Keys and Flamingo,* Chico Fernandez, Flip Pallot and Sandy Moret. All of the instructor staff are known for their tremendous angling experience and ability and a unique desire to share with someone who seeks an ultimate angling experience. The weekend sessions provide at least one instructor for every five students.

Seminars are held five or six weekends per year beginning with a Friday evening reception and ending on Sunday afternoon. For yearly schedules write to Sandy Moret, Director, Florida Keys Fly Fishing School, P.O. Box 603, Islamorada FL 33036. Phone: 305-664-5423.

FISHING GUIDES

Fishing guides may be contacted through the Florida Keys Fishing Guides Association, P.O. Box 936, Islamorada FL 33036. Rates start at $200 per day. Following is a partial listing:

George Hommell   (Guide to President George Bush)
World Wide Sportsman Inc.
MM 82.5
Islamorada FL 33036
305-664-4615

Richard Stanczyk
Bud N' Mary's Fishing Marina
MM 79.5
Islamorada FL 33036
305-664-2451

Captain Bill Knowles, Jr.
P.O. Box 836
Islamorada FL 33036
305-664-4259

Capt. Kenny Knudsen
48 Russell Lane North
Islamorada FL 33036
305-664-9281

Captain Mickey McMahan
306C Key West by the Sea
Key West FL 33040

FISHING ON YOUR OWN

For visiting anglers who trail their own small fishing craft, there are public ramps available everywhere. Numerous tackle and bait shops are available throughout the area for do-it-yourself anglers.

Small boaters fishing the reefs and wrecks will find abundant marine life on the shallow patch reefs on the Gulf side of the Keys and Everglades. On the ocean side there is excellent fishing on the coral reefs and ship wrecks which are inhabited by yellowtail, mangrove and mutton snapper, grouper and cobia. Mutton snapper up to 12 lbs have been caught by Key West reef fishermen.

In the small bays around Flamingo, the southern tip of Everglades National Park, especially Snake Bight, you have a chance for redfish, snapper or sea trout.

All boat operators should be familiar with the nautical traffic laws. These rules prevent collisions at sea and can be obtained from any U.S. Coast Guard Auxiliary.

Boats under power should never approach closer than 100 yards of another boat displaying a diver-down flag except at idle speed and with great caution.

Not all nautical hazards are marked by bouys and markers. Use charts available at dive shops, marinas and marine stores. Boaters utilizing Loran-C for navigation should recalibrate their equipment for this particular area.

A series of mooring buoys have been placed in high-use areas within the marine parks. The buoy system was developed to reduce anchor damage to the coral and provide a convenient means of securing your boats. The buoys are available on a first-come, first-served basis for everyone.

When approaching the buoys, watch for snorkelers, divers and swimmers. Approach from downwind or down-current and secure your boat to a pick-up line attached to the other end of the buoy to help in securing your boat.

FISHING REGULATIONS

As of January 1, 1990 a recreational saltwater fishing license has been required for Florida residents and nonresidents. The license is required for taking, attempting to take or possessing marine fish. These include finfish species as well as marine invertebrates. Examples of finfish are hogfish, sharks, trout, mackerel, rays, catfish, eels and tarpon.

Marine invertebrates include snails, whelks, clams, scallops, shrimp, crab lobster, sea stars, sea urchins and sea cucumbers.

With the exception of Florida residents who are fishing from shore or a pier attached to shore, salt-water fishing licenses are required of all age 16 and older. Also included are all Florida residents 16 to 65 years of age who fish from a boat, float, or place they have reached by boat, float, swimming or snorkeling.

Any person who is on a charter boat or with a licensed fishing guide is covered by their guide's license.

Crawfish and snook stamps are required for possession of either. Lobsters (crawfish) are protected year-round in some areas of Dade and Monroe counties. Sportsman's mini-season is the last full weekend prior to August 1 (two days only).

NATURE HIKES AND WALKING TOURS

For naturalists and photographers interested in native flora and wildlife, there are interpretive programs and self-guided nature trails throughout the Everglades and Keys. Park rangers provide educational and informative programs at designated natural areas. As a participant you are given unique opportunities to glimpse the wild life which inhabit the islands and wetlands. The programs include beach walks, wooded-trail hikes, bird-watching and out-island tours to observe fossilized coral or virgin tropical forests.

Combined hiking and canoe tours are offered by expedition outfitters (see Canoe chapter for listings).

EVERGLADES AND BIG CYPRESS HIKING TRAILS

The best season for hiking the trails in the Everglades is mid-December through mid-April. During summer, torrential downpours make many of the trails sloshy and difficult to hike. Precipitation can exceed 50 inches a year. After a rainfall mosquitos, sandflies and other biting insects thicken the air.

Wildlife is more difficult to spot in summer. During winter's dry season, wildlife must congregate in and around the waterholes. Many are visible from nature trails. These are holes cleared out of the Everglades limestone bed by the alligators. Fish, turtles, snails and other freshwater animals seek refuge in these life-rich holes which become feeding grounds for alligators, birds and mammals until the rains come.

Hammocks, frequently referred to in this chapter, are isolated stands of hardwoods or other like trees and plants which contrast to the surrounding plant life. You may find an island of tropical hardwoods shading orchids and ferns in the midst of a mangrove swamp. They are nature's botanical showplaces, usually formed on a ridge or elevated mound of earth. Floods, fires, and the invasion of saline waters can threaten their survival.

Ranger-Guided Hikes

Naturalists give hikes, talks, demonstrations and campfire programs during the year. Activities change daily. Ask at the visitor centers for schedules.

Many of the hiking trails in Everglades National Park take off from the Main Park Road which begins at the Main Visitor Center and ends 38 miles later at Flamingo. The park's hiking trails range from easy walks, less than one-quarter mile, to more strenuous ones up to 14 miles long. If hiking off the trails let someone know your schedule and planned route before you leave.

Watch for poisonous snakes, including coral snakes, water moccasins, diamondback and pygmy rattlers. Do not damage, remove, or disturb any plants. Like the animals, they are protected and some are poisonous—poison ivy, poison wood and manchineel. Pets are not allowed on the trails.

EVERGLADES NATIONAL PARK TRAILS

Trails marked by an asterisk are accessible for the handicapped.

The Anhinga Trail*, named for the diving bird, is less than one-half mile long. The trail starts as a paved path behind the Royal Palm Visitor's Center. From the paved walkway a narrow, raised boardwalk loops through the swamp offering a close look at alligators, herons and the anhingas which are an odd sight as they

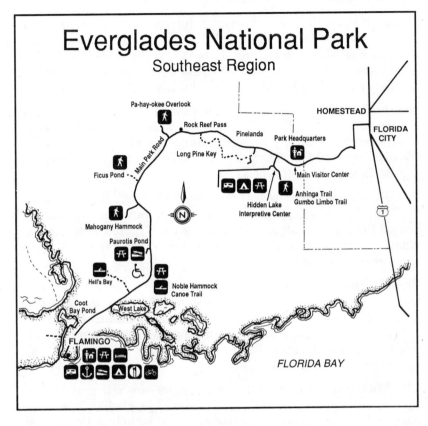

Everglades National Park
Southeast Region

Pa-hay-okee Overlook

HOMESTEAD

Rock Reef Pass

Pinelands

FLORIDA CITY

Park Headquarters

Main Park Road

Long Pine Key

Ficus Pond

Main Visitor Center

Hidden Lake
Interpretive Center

Anhinga Trail
Gumbo Limbo Trail

N

Mahogany Hammock

Paurotis Pond

Hell's Bay

Noble Hammock
Canoe Trail

Coot
Bay Pond

West Lake

FLAMINGO

FLORIDA BAY

flatten themselves out against the bushes to dry. This trail is the nearest to the Main Visitor's Center and offers the best opportunity to see several species of wildlife close up. Residents include alligators, turtles, fish, marsh rabbits and many birds, including anhingas, herons, egrets, and purple gallinules. Taylor Slough, a freshwater, marshy river supplies water for plants and animals throughout the dry winter season.

The Gumbo Limbo Trail*, winds for one-half mile through a hardwood hammock of tropical trees and smaller plants. The trail starts behind the Royal Palm Visitor's Center, adjacent to the Anhinga Trail. There are royal palms, gumbo limbo trees, wild coffee, and lush aerial gardens of ferns and orchids.

At Long Pine Key, a network of interconnecting trails runs through seven miles of the Pinelands, a diverse pine forest. About 200 types of plants, including 30 found nowhere else on Earth, grow under the pine canopy. Whitetail deer, opossums, raccoons and the endangered Florida panther live here.

Shark Valley* is a 15-mile trail into the heart of the Everglades prairie. It lies off U.S. 41, the Tamiami Trail. Here, at the head-waters for Shark River you can see alligators, otters, wood storks, snakes, deer, and fish. There is a 50-ft observation tower for viewing the Everglades wilderness.

The Pineland Trail* is less than one-half mile. It begins near the Main Visitor's Center and is the best place to see the shallow bed of limestone that underlies the area. Exposed limestone is dimpled with solution holes formed when rainwater and the organic acid from plant matter mix.

The Pa-hay-okee Overlook Trail, less than one-quarter mile, leads to an observation tower where you can view the "river of grass"—the true glades that gave the park its name. Sawgrass, Everglades beardgrass, and arrowhead grow here. From the trail you may spot a red-shouldered hawk, vultures, alligators, pygmy rattlesnakes or king snakes.

The Mahogany Hammock Trail*, under one-half mile, enters the cooler, damp environment of a dark, jungle-like hardwood hammock. Here massive mahogany trees, including the largest living specimen in the United States, thrive. Beside the mahogany trees are paurotis palms. Look up for zebra butterflies, airplants, orchids and huge spider webs that are suspended from tree branches.

The West Lake Trail* begins on the south side of the main road 31 miles from the Main Visitor's Center. The half-mile trail winds through mangrove trees edging the large brackish lake. It continues past Long Lake and ends at Alligator Creek. Four types of mangroves, red, black, white and buttonwood, grow in this region where the glades meet saltwater. This region is a nursery for fish crabs, shrimp and spiny lobsters.

Flamingo Hiking Trails

Main Park Road

Coot Bay Pond   Mrazek Pond

Bear Lake

FLORIDA BAY

N

0   1   2

1. Snake Bight
2. Rowdy Bend
3. Christian Point
4. Bear Lake
5. Eco Pond
6. Guy Bradley
7. Bayshore Loop
8. Coastal Prairie

FLAMINGO AREA TRAILS

Snake Bight Trail leads through 1 3/5 miles of tropical hardwood hammock edging Snake Bight Channel. This is a densely wooded, shady, unpaved trail. There is good birdwatching from the short boardwalk at the end of the trail where large alligators are also spotted.

Rowdy Bend is a 2 1/2-mile, old road bed that twists through buttonwood forest and open coastal prairie. It ends at junction with Snake Bight Trail.

Bear Lake Trail starts at the Main Park Road and leads through 1 3/5 miles of dense hardwood hammock ending at Bear Lake. This is an excellent habitat for woodland birds.

Christian Point, a short way from the Flamingo Visitor's Center, is a rustic path which begins in dense buttonwood forest and ends at the coastal prairie along the Snake Bight shore.

Coastal Prairie Trail, once used by cotton pickers and fishermen, begins at the "C" Loop in the Flamingo Campground. Length

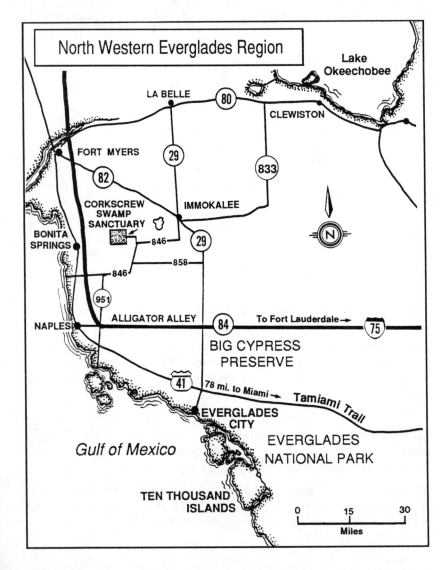

is 7 1/2 miles one way. A backcountry permit is required for camping along the trail.

Bayshore Loop meanders for two miles along the shore of Florida Bay. It begins at Coastal Prairie Trail Head at the back of Loop "C" in the Flamingo Campground. Veer left at the trail junction to the bay.

Eco Pond is a half-mile stroll around a freshwater pond. There is a viewing platform from which herons and other wading birds may be photographed.

Guy Bradley is a scenic one-mile shortcut between the Flamingo Campground and Visitor's Center.   It runs along the shore of Florida Bay. The trail is named for a game warden who lost his life defending nesting birds from plume hunters. In the late 1800's egret and heron plumes were in big demand by the millinery industry for decorating ladies' hats.

BIG CYPRESS

The Florida Trail is a 29-mile, marked hiking trail that crosses Big Cypress National Park between Alligator Alley and the Tamiami Trail. It is closed to all vehicles. Watch for muck soil, sharp-edged pinnacle rock and holes, poisonous plants and snakes. There are two primitive camp grounds with drinking water. Check with a park ranger before you begin a hiking trip. The trail wanders through cypress swamp and pinelands.

For additional information contact: Big Cypress National Preserve, Star Route Box 110, Ochopee FL 33943. Phone: 813-695-2000 or 813-262-1066.

THE CORKSCREW SWAMP SANCTUARY

The National Audubon Society's Corkscrew Swamp Sanctuary contains one of the largest stands of mature bald cypress trees in the nation. It is also the most scenic of the Everglades trails. Here you can stroll through a natural cathedral formed by giant bald cypress trees on a boardwalk loop 1 3/4 miles long and enjoy an unforgettable remnant of an undisturbed primeval forest. Pick up the illustrated self-guiding tour booklet that describes the native plants and animals that may be seen. Members of the staff are on hand to answer questions and explain the relationships between water, wildlife and man. Nesting woodstorks, bald eagles, bobcats, alligators, and otters are frequently seen. Mosquitofish eat the mosquitos and eliminate the need for repellent. No pets. Wheelchairs are available. Groups may request, in advance, a naturalist. The sanctuary is located 1 1/2 miles from County Road 846. The Sanctuary Road entrance (County Road 849) is 14 miles from Immokalee, 21 miles from Route 41, and 15 miles from Interstate 75, Exit 17. The Visitor's Center and Boardwalk Trail is open from 9 am to 5 pm daily. Admission $5. Children under six free. Audubon members $3. For information write Corkscrew Swamp Sanctuary, Route 6, Box 1875-A, Naples Fl 33964. Phone: 813-657-3771.

COLLIER SEMINOLE STATE PARK

To reach this park turn right off the Tamiami Trail about 17 miles west of the Route 29 intersection. The 6,423-acre park is named for the late Barron Collier, a pioneer developer in Collier Country, and for the Seminole Indians who still live nearby. The county began the development of the park before it became a state park in 1947.

A self-guided trail winds through 6 1/2 miles of pine flatwood and cypress swamps. A primitive campsite is provided for overnight excursions. There are also two sites for tent and RV camping.

Some of the final campaigns of the Second Seminole War were conducted near here, and a replica of a blockhouse used by U.S. forces and local defenders during that era has been erected in the park. A "walking dredge" used to build the Tamiami Trail in the 1920's is also on display.

There is a boat basin on the Blackwater River which flows through the park. Canoe trail and rentals available. Handicapped accessible. For more information contact: Collier Seminole State Park, Rt. 4, Box 848, Naples FL 33961. Phone: 813-394-3397.

FLORIDA KEYS NATURE HIKES

John Pennekamp State Park *, located at MM 102.5, has two short nature trails. One leads through a tropical hammock, home to raccoons and birds. It starts at the parking lot across from the Visitor's Center. The other is an elevated boardwalk through mangroves where you may view resident wading birds—herons, cormorants and coots. The mangrove trail begins in the parking lot across from the Picnic Pavilion. The park offers ranger-guided interpretive programs and water-sport facilities.

Lignumvitae Key*, a 280-acre island on the Gulf side of Islamorada, is a virgin tropical forest accessible by charter boat. Isolated in time and space relative to the other keys, Lignumvitae Key was bought by a financier named William Matheson who built a four-bedroom, coral-rock house on it in 1919, but left the rest of the island alone except for a small clearing and boat dock. The State of Florida acquired the key in 1972 and made it a protected state botanical site. Today the house serves as a visitor's center. State park rangers conduct guided tours three times daily, Thursday through Monday.

On the tour, you'll see several lignumvitae trees, mahogany, strangler fig, poisonwood, pigeon plum and gumbo limbo trees.

Only 50 people are allowed on the key at one time—25 on the nature trail and 25 in the clearing. Walking shoes and mosquito repellent are recommended. Book a trip at the MM 78.5 boat ramp. Phone: 305-664-4815.

Indian Key State Historical Site* is a 12-acre island on the ocean side of Islamorada. There are ruins of a wreckers' village on the island and numerous sisal plants planted by famed botanist, Dr. Henry Perrine. The village was burned down by the Indians in 1840.

Book a guided, walking tour at the MM 78.5 boat ramp. Call the Florida Park Service at 305-664-4815 for schedules.

Long Key State Park *, at MM 67.5, supports an abundant wading-bird population which can readily be observed from the park nature trail. The main trail originates on the ocean side, near

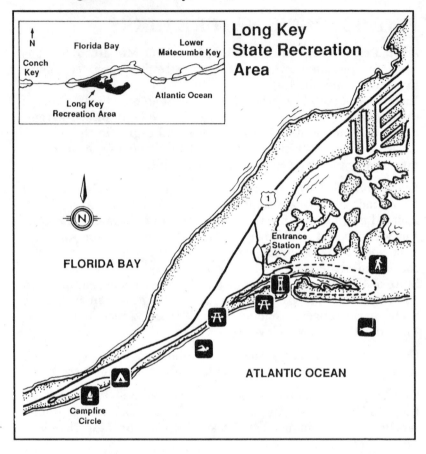

the observation tower. It winds through natural areas of the island, along the beach and along a boardwalk over a
mangrove-lined lagoon. Signs are found along the boardwalk
which interpret the lagoon. Park rangers present campfire programs and lead guided walks year-round. The park opens at 8 am
and closes at sunset.

Crane Point Hammock*, located at MM 50, is a 63-acre environmental and archaeological site. The tract is especially significant because it contains the last virgin palm hammock in
North America. The property also contains evidence of

pre-Columbian and prehistoric Indian artifacts and was once the site of an entire Bahamian village. Also on the grounds are an "Indian-and-hurricane-proof" home built with two-foot-thick walls in the late 1800's. Other artifacts dating from the same era have been found on the property.

Key Deer, Big Pine Key

You enter the sanctuary through the Museum of Natural History of the Florida Keys. It features 20 major exhibits and a half dozen rotating displays covering the evolution of geography, botany and zoology in the Keys.

The trail is a one-quarter mile tour of a pit exposing ancient coral fossils, rare hardwoods, native palms and red mangroves. Crane Point Hammock and its natural history museum are open 9 am to 5 pm, Wednesday through Monday. Phone: 305-743-9100.

Bahia Honda State Park*, at MM 36.5, has always been a favorite stopping point for motorists traveling the Overseas Highway. At the far end of Sandspur Beach, oceanside, a nature trail follows the shore of a tidal lagoon, then goes through a coastal strand hammock and back along the beach. Bahia Honda has a number of plants that are not often found on the other islands. Among the rarer species are the satinwood tree, spiny catesbaea and dwarf morning glory.

The bird life of Bahia Honda includes beautiful and rare species such as the white-crowned pigeon, great white heron, roseate spoonbill, reddish egret, osprey, brown pelican and least tern.

Guided walks are provided with special interpretive programs available to groups by reservation.

Big Pine Key Walking Trail is located 1 1/2 miles north of the intersection of Key Deer Boulevard and Watson Boulevard. It is two-thirds mile long and winds through typical Big Pine Key habitat consisting of slash pine and palms. At one point the trail touches Watson Hammock, a unique hardwood area which is also habitat for a variety of tree cactus and a species of prickly pear not seen anywhere else in the world. The trail is within the Key Deer Refuge, home of tiny deer measuring 24 to 32 inches at the shoulder and weighing 45 to 75 pounds. Fawns weigh two to four pounds with a hoof the size of a thumb nail. Rangers ask that you don't feed the deer.

Nearby is an old rock quarry, the Blue Hole, that is the largest body of freshwater in the Florida Keys. One or more alligators reside in the quarry.

THE PELICAN PATH

A Walking Tour of Old Key West

In Key West, one soon forgets he or she is in the United States, as Spanish is heard drifting from porch to porch, while the conchs, the natives of English strain, tell in cockney accent stories of anything from marlin to mermaids. Here, one forgets the cares of city life. The sun is always warm, the sky is always clear and just a little way down the street is the most beautiful sea in the world, of a pure turquoise color that deepens to emerald on the horizon.

KEY WEST ARCHITECTURE

As the most historic city in South Florida, Key West owes much of its charm to its distinctive architecture. According to the Executive Director of the National Trust for Historic Preservation, "Some of these quaint and charming houses are to be found in no other area of the country." Their history goes back to the early beginnings of Key West when the first settlers came to the island. These pioneers were from the eastern seaboard of the United States, the Bahama Islands, Cuba and Europe. Many of the old houses in Key West reflect this delightful mixture of nationalities which has created a feeling described as old world atmosphere. Of these styles or types of buildings the one most typical and distinctively Key West is known as "Conch" or Bahama. Built of wood by ships' carpenters, their simple, clean lines have the same balance

Material from the Pelican Path Guide is reproduced with permission of the Old Island Restoration Foundation, Inc.

and grace found in a fine sailing ship. They were built to withstand high winds and a tropical climate. Their wide porches have slender square columns which support the main roof and in some instances windows under the eaves open onto the porches. All the windows were protected by shutters or "blinds" which allowed light and air into the high-ceilinged rooms, yet kept out the hot tropic sun. The high peaked roofs were designed to catch the maximum amount of rain water which was stored in great cisterns. On the small houses hatches, similar to those found on a ship, when open allowed air and light into the attic bedrooms. The cupolas or "widow's walks" on many of the larger buildings were used as a lookout to scan the nearby reefs for ships that had run aground. These sturdy houses have a classic simplicity at times relieved by the addition of lacy woodwork or delicately-turned spindles on the porch rails.

Nearly all the early buildings were made of wood; however, some were constructed of stone quarried on the island. Two examples are to be seen on Old Mallory Square; others are the Old Stone Methodist Church and the Hemingway House. With the exception of Fort Taylor, brick was not used to any great extent until after the fire of 1886 when half the town was destroyed.

Buildings of various styles, material and periods are to be seen throughout the island. Their architecture is often reminiscent of other places but somehow there is a difference. In this difference, you will recognize the charm that is found only in "Old Key West."

THE PELICAN PATH

Colorful Pelican signs mark the route on this unique walking tour of Key West's historic section. Plaques on buildings of special interest are also numbered. Developed by the Old Island Restoration Foundation, it has been planned so you may visit the quaint older section of the city and learn more about the buildings and their history.

The asterisks are used to designate the following: * Historic Markers; ** Historic American Buildings. These buildings were included in the survey conducted in 1967-1968 by the National Park Service and Old Island Restoration Foundation. Copies of the sur-

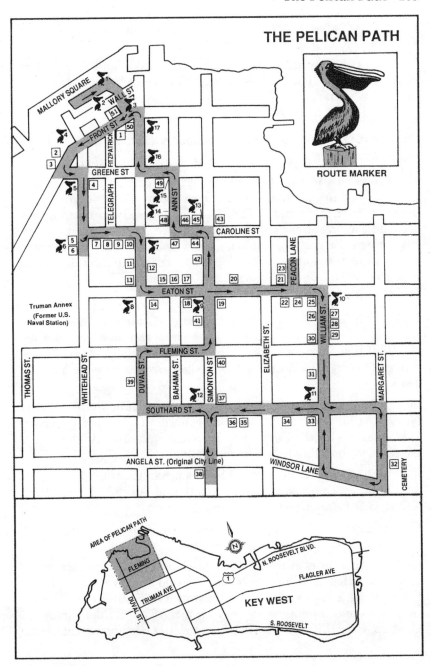

vey are available at the Monroe Country Public Library in Key West and the Library of Congress.

The Tour begins at the headquarters of the Old Island Restoration Foundation in Old Mallory Square. Follow the arrows on the map to keep on course.

Turn right at Pelican 1.

Continue to Pelican 2 at the Mallory Square Exit.

Continue on Wolfson Lane: Turn right on Front St. at Pelican 3.

1— **Sawyer Building**, 400 Front St. Erected after the fire of 1886 by a Bahamian merchant. It is one of the many structures built during this era by immigrant Irish brick layers from Boston. The second floor was at one time used by the U.S. District court. **Front Street** was the early commercial district of Key West. Ships from all ports of the world docked here and large warehouses stored goods salvaged from the numerous shipwrecks.

Cross Whitehead St. to Clinton Place to Pelican 4.

Clinton Place, Greene and Whitehead Sts. Within this triangle is a memorial shaft honoring the Union troops who died here during the Civil War, most of whom were victims of Yellow Fever. It was named for DeWitt Clinton who was the Governor of New York in 1828.

2— * ** **Coast Guard Building**, Front St. Built in 1856 for a Navy Coaling Station, it was later used in the Civil War as Headquarters for the East Coast Blockade Squadron. As the oldest government building it is known as "Bldg. 1."

3—** **Old Post Office**, Front St. This ornamental brick building was built by the government in 1891 and was used as a Post Office, U.S. Court House and Customs House.

Continue around Clinton Place, turning right on Whitehead St. at Pelican 5.

4—* ** **Audubon House**, 205 Whitehead St. The preservation and restoration of this exceptionally fine old home was responsible for creating a city-wide interest in preserving other buildings of historical and architectural significance. The former home of Captain John H. Geiger, it is now a museum housing an extensive collection of original works by John James Audubon. Period furnishings re-create the era when the naturalist-painter visited the island in 1832.

Whitehead Street. Of the five military roads built by Commodore David Porter, only this one remains. For many years no other road transversed the full length of the island.

On your right is the President's Gate. This ceremonial gate which leads to the "Little White House" was opened only for Presidents and other international dignitaries.

5,6—Truman Annex, 324, 326 Whitehead St. There had been a shortage of suitable officers' housing at the Naval Station from the 1870's and a plan was submitted in 1898 to build Quarters C and D on the 300 block of Whitehead. They are significant as examples of early 20th century domestic architecture designed by Navy architects to blend with the character of the surrounding private residences of Key West. In 1905 finishing touches, such as lattice work, porch screens and painting, brought the total cost to $6,000 for both houses. Extensive restoration in 1989 brought these homes back to life, providing a link between old Key West and the evolution of the new Truman Annex.

Turn Right on Caroline St. at Pelican 6.

7—Airways House, 301 Whitehead St. This building originally stood on the waterfront where it was used as offices for Aero-Marine Airways. The first international air mail route between Key West and Havana was established November 1, 1920. In October 1927 the route was taken over by Pan American Airways and in January of the following year six passengers made the 90-mile trip in one hour and 20 minutes.

8—Captain George Cary House, 410 Caroline St. The original section of this handsome dwelling was torn down; however, the old chimney remains and forms a part of the present garden. The existing house was built in the mid-1850's.

9—Judge W. Hunt Harris House, 425 Caroline St. Built toward the end of the Spanish American War, the building was utilized during that period by the Navy. Judge Harris served in the State Legislature and Senate and was, at one time, a Lieutenant Governor of Florida.

10—J.Y. Porter House, 429 Caroline St. Dr. J. Y. Porter II was born here in 1847 and died in the same room 80 years later. The Doctor's extensive research in Yellow Fever established our present quarantine laws. In recognition of this, he was made Florida's first Public Health Officer.

Turn right on Duval St. at Pelican 7.

11—Oldest House/Wreckers Museum, 322 Duval St. Records and deed books indicate that this house was built on Whitehead St. in 1829, then moved to its present location in 1832. It is now owned by the State of Florida and is maintained and managed by the Old Island Restoration Foundation. Of special interest are the three upstairs dormer windows graduating in size and the cook house and garden in the rear.

12—Woman's Club, 319 Duval St. This beautifully proportioned house was built in 1892 by the first manager of the Inter-Ocean Telegraph Office. Since 1941 it has been the home of the Key West Woman's Club.

13—Patterson House, 336 Duval St. Built by Alexander Patterson, it was occupied by Mr. and Mrs. William Pickney and their children. The first private school was conducted here in 1842 by Mrs. Pickney's sister, Mrs. Passalogue, a French lady of rare interest and attainments. The next occupants were the Baldwins, an aristocratic British family who traced their ancestry to Lord Nelson and Sir Robert Walpole.

Turn left on Eaton St. at Pelican 8.

14—St. Paul's Church, 401 Duval. This is the oldest Episcopal church in the Diocese of South Florida. The first service was held here on Christmas Day in 1832. The present church, erected in 1916, is the fourth to be built on this site.

15—Warren House, 511 Eaton St. The residence of the Warren family for over 80 years, this home also was the office of Dr. William Richard Warren, an early island physician. It also features the tallest cistern in Key West.

16—Skelton House, 517 Eaton St.

17—Alvarez House, 523 Eaton St.   These two lovely homes reflect the unique warmth and ambiance of Old Key West.

18—**Otto House**, 534 Eaton St. Built by Thomas Osgood Otto, Sr. and completed just before the turn of the century, it is of West Indian-Colonial-Victorian architecture and is one of the few remaining homes of this type on the island. The original French wallpaper was mounted on linen so that during a hurricane, if the house rocked, the paper would not crack.

Cross Simonton St. at Pelican 9.

19—**Old Stone Methodist Church**, 600 Eaton St. This handsome church, shaded by a giant Spanish laurel tree, was built in 1877 of stone quarried on the island. It is the oldest religious building in Key West.

20—**Peter A. Williams House**, 619 Eaton St. The United States Marshal who lived here dynamited his home in the 1886 fire in an attempt to stop the holocaust. The present house was built by him after the fire.

Eaton Street was named for John Henry Eaton, a United States Senator and later a member of President Andrew Jackson's cabinet. His marriage to Peggy O'Neil created a scandal in Washington. Later, Jackson appointed the controversial Mr. Eaton Governor of Florida.

Continue on Eaton, crossing Elizabeth St.

21—**Saunders House**, 709 Eaton St. Restored in 1975, this pre-Victorian home was originally built around 1850 by Eliza and William Uriah Saunders of New Plymouth, Green Turtle Cay in the Bahamas.

22—**Richard Peacon House**, 712 Eaton St. Richard Peacon, owner of the town's largest grocery store then at 800 Fleming and now known as William Fleming House, built the house between 1892 and 1899. Often called the "Octagon House," its stark symmetry makes it an architectural standout. Restored and refurbished by the late designer Angelo Donghia, the house was purchased by Calvin Klein in the 1980's for close to $1 million and later re-sold.

23—**The Susan Peacon House**, 320 Peacon Lane. Peacon Lane was formerly called Grunt Bone Alley. Built about 1848 and lived in by the Peacons for 100 years. Restored in 1972, this small conch cottage has a well established characteristic conch garden.

24—Filer House, 724 Eaton St. Built in 1885 and considered one of the classic homes on the island, it is an outstanding example of Bahamian architecture with Victorian influence. Note how the columns are enriched by the ornamental trim.

25—Bahama House (I), 730 Eaton St. In 1847, John Bartium and his brother-in-law Richard Roberts of Green Turtle Cay in the Bahamas, dismantled their homes and brought them to Key West. In 1855 Bartium built the famous clipper ship Stephen R. Mallory. She is said to have been the only clipper ever to be built in Florida.

Turn right on William St. at Pelican 10.

26—Bahama House (II), 408 William St. This was the home of Richard Roberts, one of the early settlers of the Florida Keys. Unlike any other house on the island, the double verandas extend the entire length of the building. The handplaned pine siding varies in width and has a unique beading on the lower edges.

27—Gideon Lowe House, 409 William St. The first part of the house was built in the early 1840's and the second section was added in the 1870's. It reflects an outstanding version of Classic Revival architecture.

28—Island City House, 411 William St. Built in the early 1900's it was operated as a hotel until the late forties. Condemned by the City, it was saved by the present owners and has been handsomely restored.

29—Russell House, 415 William St. This lovely old house built at the turn of the century depicts the charm and grace of an earlier age.

30—Fleming Street Methodist Church, 729 Fleming St. The original church was built in 1884 by dissenting members of the mother church who objected to instrumental music. Having been destroyed by the hurricane of 1909, the present concrete structure was completed in 1912. Because many members of the congregation were seamen who wore short jackets, it became known as "the short jacket Methodist church."

Continue on William St. crossing Fleming St.

Fleming Street. Named for John W.C. Fleming, a native of

England and a business partner of John Simonton. Fleming hoped to develop the salt industry here, but his death in 1832 ended the project.

31—Charles Roberts House, 512 Fleming St. Built in the late 1800's this charming home follows every rule for pleasant island living.

Turn left on Southard St. at Pelican 11, then right on Margaret St.

32—Key West Cemetery. Reminiscent of New Orleans and Galveston graveyards, the unique above-ground vaults are described by Key West poet James Merrill as "whitewashed hope chests." You'll see the *U.S. Maine* monument, a headstone proclaiming "I Told You I Was Sick," chiselled poems, hand carved angels and glass mausoleums with statuary. Traditional cornet band funeral parades still occur in the cemetery which was relocated from near the Southernmost Point on Whitehead St. after the devastating 1846 hurricane.

Turn right on Windsor Lane, then right on William St., then left on Southard St.

33—William Albury House, 730 Southard St. One of the oldest homes in Key West, it is also considered one of the most interesting. It has double porches on three sides and is crowned with a widow's walk.

34—John Albury House, 708 Southard St. Purchased from the Albury family by Cleveland Dillon in the late 1900's, the house remained in the family until the 1960's.

35—John Lowe, Jr. House, 620 Southard St. This residence was enlarged as the family and their fortune grew. It is typical of the mid-19th century homes built by successful Key West merchants with significant features that include wide porches and a widow's walk. Mr. Lowe was the owner of one of the largest sponging fleets in Florida.

36—Benjamin Curry House, 610 Southard St. The property was purchased in 1856 from Pardon Greene who was one of the four original owners of the island. This story-and-a-half house has been the home of six generations of the Curry family.

37—William C. Lowe House, 603 Southard St. Built after 1865, the house remained in the family until 1942. It is of classic design and an outstanding example of restoration.

Turn left on Simonton St. at Pelican 12.

Simonton St. Named for an American businessman, John W. Simonton who bought the island of Key West from the Spanish owner Juan Pablo Salas in 1821 for $2,000.

38—The Peggy Mills House and Garden, 516 Angela St. Built prior to 1889, this house was totally renovated in 1982. The gardens, created by Peggy Mills, furniture store owner and plant lover, were started in 1930, and for 50 years Peggy never stopped adding to them. Internationally known for its varied botanical collection, the gardens also feature antique tinajones (Cuban water jugs weighing one ton empty) and winding pathways of century old brick.

Return to Southard St., turn left, then right on Duval St.

39—San Carlos Opera House, 516 Duval St. The San Carlos Institute was dedicated in 1871 as a political and social center for the Cuban community. The Spanish language was taught in the only public school in the U.S. maintained by a foreign government. A splendid example of Cuban architecture with beautiful majolica tiles from Spain in the interior lobby. A school, an opera house, the Cuban consulate and a movie theatre have all been located in the structure. In 1988, the San Carlos was awarded over a million dollars for restoration and it reopened in 1989 after being abandoned and closed for several years.

Turn right on Fleming St.

40—John Haskins Building (Marquesa Hotel), 600 Fleming. Built prior to 1889, this structure is now a small luxury hotel which received the 1988 First Place Winner for Historic Preservation. It has been a drugstore, car dealership and the first home of Fausto's grocery now located in the next block.

41—William R. Kerr House, 410 Simonton St. Built in 1876 by the owner, the house shows the strong influence of Downings' Carpenter Gothic design in the roof style, vergeboards and porch ornaments. Mr. Kerr, a prominent architect, built many of the important public structures on the island.

42—Simonton Court, 320 Simonton St. The interesting weathered appearance of this old cigar factory was produced by staining the wood. It has large tropical gardens, pools and the original workers' cottages in the rear. A private oasis in the middle of a busy area.

43—* Richard Kemp House, unpainted, 601 Caroline St. An excellent example of Bahamian architecture in its purest form. Its simplicity of lines and styling with fine proportions and balance reflect the craftsmanship of ships' carpenters. The Kemp family migrated from the Bahamas to Key West shortly after the island was settled. William Kemp introduced the sponge industry to Key West and sold the first shipment of Florida sponges in New York.

44—Delaney House, 532 Caroline St. Built around 1889, it was owned by John J. Delaney, a merchant in the clothing business. This handsome structure has been used for various business and professional offices but has retained its original architecture.

45—George Bartlum House, 531 Caroline St. Built in the mid-1800's in three stages, it was finished in 1888. President and Mrs. Harry Truman were frequent guests in this home.

46—Bott House, 529 Caroline St. This distinctive house is one of the few brick homes in Key West.

47—George B. Patterson House, 522 Caroline St. Mr. Patterson's father, Col. Alexander Patterson, came to Key West from Connecticut in the 1820's. The design of the house reflects the Queen Anne style of architecture.

Turn right on Ann St. at Pelican 14.

48—Milton Curry House, 511 Caroline St. Built in 1905, this house is a copy of a Newport cottage which the young couple had admired. A wide graceful porch surrounds the house on three sides. Of special interest is the elegant design and detail on the verandas and under the eaves.

49—Old City Hall, 512 Greene St. Built in 1891 on the same site as the former City Hall destroyed in the 1886 fire. This historic landmark is presently being restored by the Historic Florida Keys Preservation Board, Old Island Restoration Foundation, the City of Key West and its generous citizens.

Turn left on Greene St. at Pelican 15. Turn right on Duval St.

Duval St. has for many years been the city's main shopping and entertainment center. It was named for Florida's first Territorial Governor, William Pope Duval.

50—Florida First National Bank, Front and Duval Sts. This establishment has been in operation since 1891. The original building shows strong Spanish influence in the beautiful and intricate brick work as well as in the ornate balcony. On display in the lobby is part of the famous solid gold table service made by Tiffany.

Turn left on Front St. at Pelican 17.

51—Harbor House, 423 Front St. The first Bank of Key West built on this site in 1885 was destroyed by fire the following year. Rebuilt shortly thereafter, the brick building was gutted again by fire in 1984. It is currently being restored. The structure is reminiscent of the architecture found in New Orleans.

PARASAILING

Parasailing combines the thrill of hang gliding with the excitement of parachuting. It's much safer, requires no training and you don't need to jump out of an airplane or from a towering cliff. The new custom parasailing boats allow you to take off and land right on the deck.

Once you buy your ticket and climb aboard, the boat moves to an open-space, over-water area. Next you are strapped into a life jacket and special harness. The deck hand slackens your safety line and, within seconds, you are whisked 400 feet aloft. The ride lasts about 15 minutes. As the powerboat pulls you across a panorama of coral reefs, mangrove islands and coves, you ride a column of air and see the world from a birdseye view. Like a kite, you are always connected to the boat by a safety line. As long as the boat is moving, the relative wind keeps you up. When you wish to come down, the boat slows up. You settle toward earth and are reeled back aboard the boat by an electric winch. Photo and video opportunities are magnificent.

Don't worry if the boat runs out of gas and the winch motor breaks. Keep in mind that big nylon apparatus you are hanging from is a parachute. If all fails you will float gently down and splash into the sea. Wear a bathing suit.

When you parasail with Carlos Crucet at Holiday Isle, getting wet is part of the fun. His 28-foot custom-designed, parasail boat is kept in tip-top shape, but his patrons demand an intentional dip in the sea to cool off. After 15 minutes close to Florida's sun you'll want one too. You can sign up for a trip with Carlos on the Holiday Isle beach at Mojo's Shack (664-5390) or at the huge "parasailing" sign on the north end of the beach. Six people can go in the boat at once. Spectators ride along for a nominal fee. A special tandem-parasail set-up allows a parent to take a small child along. Arrangements for the handicapped are available.

In Key West you can lift off at Island Parasail (294-7836), 700 Front St., Slip 4. Or stop by Sunset Watersports (296-2552 or 294-1987), located at both Higgs and Smathers Beach.

Winch Parasailing offers rides at Cheeca Lodge, MM 82 (664-4651 ext. 551).

Parasailing in Key Largo is offered weekends at Caribbean Watersports, located at the Italian Fisherman beach complex, MM 104 (451-3113). Arrangements for a ride can be made at the watersports shack on the Sheraton's beach, bayside, MM 97.

Prices for a 15-minute ride start at $45. Light wind and calm sea conditions are necessary.

SCUBA

Spectacular coral reefs, offshore to Florida's Keys, attract nearly a million sport divers each year. Patches of finger-like, spur and groove reefs parallel the islands from Key Biscayne to Key West and are inhabited by over 500 varieties of fish and corals. Shallow depths, ideal for underwater video and still photography, range from just below the surface to an average maximum of 40 feet.

What you Need

A scuba certification card (C-card) is required to join dive boat trips or obtain air fills. Dive operators may request a look at your logbook before signing you on a trip. Without one, you may be asked to take a check-out dive. An advanced scuba certification is required for dives on the deep wrecks, *Duane* and *Bibb*.

Many dive shops offer resort courses. You take a lesson in a pool then an introductory dive on a shallow reef with an instructor. Refresher courses are available too.

Gear

During winter, when ocean temperatures average 70-75°F, you'll find a shorty, one-eighth-inch wetsuit comfortable. Water temperatures climb to 85°F in summer, making a wetsuit unnecessary. A safe-second regulator is encouraged, but not mandatory. Standard gear—bouyancy compensators, weight belts, weights, mask, knife, snorkel, camera and video equipment—may all be rented at any dive shop. Boaters may rent small craft at any of the marinas.

Weather

Diving in Florida's Keys is weather-dependent. You can go out to the reefs in the morning after a storm and find visibility as low as 25 ft and return in the afternoon to calm seas and visibility in excess of 100 ft. The best months are usually October through June. Because the reefs are fairly shallow (most 45 ft or less) winds that churn up the seas may cause lowered visibility.

When storms rule out trips to the outer reefs, visit the Content Keys, a sheltered area which is almost always calm, located on the Gulf side of Marathon.

CEDAM

Specialized study programs and unique scientific expeditions such as collecting artifacts from ancient shipwrecks for museums or mapping underwater terrain are offered by CEDAM, a non-profit organization. For information on Florida Keys trips call or write: CEDAM International, Fox Road, Croton-on-Hudson NY 10520. Phone: 914-271-5365.

Buddies

Need a dive buddy? Divers Exchange International offers a unique service which will match you up with a fellow diver in the Keys, or anywhere. Write to Wendy Church, DEI, 37 W. Cedar St., Boston MA. 02114. Phone: 617-723-2960, fax 617-227-8145.

The Florida Keys National Marine Sanctuary

After three freighters grounded on the reefs in 1989, destroying acres of the tiny coral reef organisms, President Bush signed into law a bill designed to protect a 3,000-square-mile stretch of Florida Keys land and sea. The area known as The Florida Keys National Marine Sanctuary contains the entire strand of Keys barrier reefs on the Atlantic and Gulf sides of the islands. Freighter traffic close to shore is prohibited, providing a safe "cushion" area between keels and corals.

The sanctuary, managed by the National Oceanographic and Atmospheric Administration, also encompasses, and dwarfs, two previous federal preserves in the Keys, the Looe Key National Marine Sanctuary and the Key Largo National Marine Sanctuary. In contrast to the new 3,500-square-mile sanctuary, the Looe Key sanctuary is 5.32 square miles and the Key Largo sanctuary is 100 square miles.

Parasailing, Islamorada

Swimming with dolphins, Theatre of the Sea, Islamorada

Soft corals, Key Largo

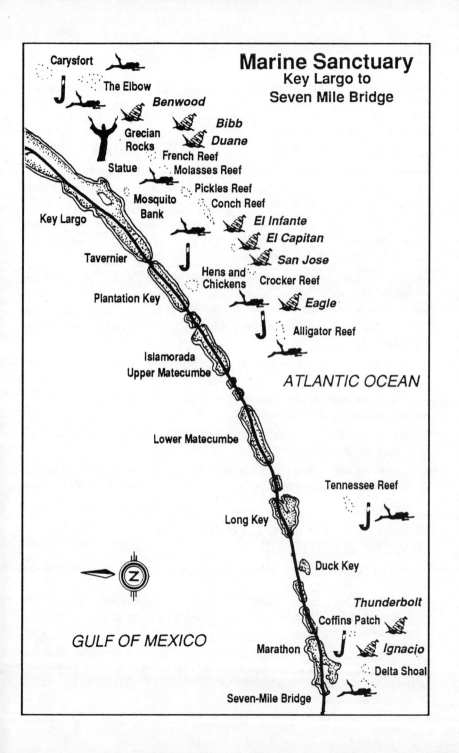

Within the sanctuary, spearfishing, wearing gloves and anchoring on the coral are prohibited.

Reef Etiquette

Do not allow your hands, knees, tank or fins to contact the coral. Just touching coral causes damage to the fragile polyps.

Spearfishing in the sanctuary is not allowed. This is one reason the fish are so friendly that you can almost reach out and touch them.

Hand feeding of fish is discouraged, especially food unnatural to them. Besides the risk of bodily injury, such activity changes the natural behavior of the fish.

Hook and line fishing is allowed. Applicable size, catch limits and seasons must be observed.

Spiny lobster may be captured during the season except in the Core Area of the Looe Key Sanctuary. Number and size regulations must be followed.

Corals, shells, starfish and other animals cannot be removed from the Sanctuary.

Regulations prohibiting littering and discharge of any substances except chum are strictly enforced.

Fines are imposed for running aground or damaging coral. Historical artifacts are protected.

The red and white dive flag must be flown while diving or snorkeling. Boats must go slow enough to leave no wake within 100 yds of a dive flag.

BISCAYNE NATIONAL PARK MARINE SANCTUARY

Biscayne National Park Marine Sanctuary is gaining interest from those who enjoy an uncrowded environment. Vietnam veteran and Audubon activist, Ed Davidson is largely responsible for masterminding a successful fight to save this Northern Key Largo area from future development.

The major groups of coral reef patches are two to three miles offshore and require a boat for access. Diving in Biscayne is relatively new, with many virgin areas open to discover. Good visibility and pristine reefs are attracting divers to the park.

JOHN PENNEKAMP
CORAL REEF STATE PARK

John Pennekamp Coral Reef State Park has long been the most popular diving area in Florida. The park is named for the late John D. Pennekamp (1897 -1978), editor of the Miami Herald, who fostered the idea of reef preservation and, with fellow ecologists, raised enough money to purchase the southwest edge of Largo Sound for a park headquarters site. The park, a part of the Florida Keys National Marine Sanctuary, consists of 100 square miles of undersea reefs and 75 land acres as a haven not only for divers and snorkelers, but also campers, bird watchers, fishermen and sunbathers. This, the world's first underwater state park, was formed in 1960 at the urging of a group of marine biologists and naturalists who were concerned about the destruction of the United States' only continental living reef system. In the past corals and conch shells had been harvested and bleached for souvenirs; spear fishermen had killed angelfish and anything else that moved underwater. Today, concern continues as environmentalists fight overdevelopment and accompanying ocean pollutants.

Dive shop signs and billboards offering reef trips line the highway throughout Key Largo. Boat trips to the best dive sites takes from 15-30 minutes depending on sea and wind conditions.

Dive Sites

The park's most popular dive, and perhaps the one which symbolizes the area, is "the statue", a nine-foot bronze replica of **"Christ of the Abyss"**, created by sculptor Guido Galletti for placement in the Mediterranean Sea. The statue was given to the Underwater Society of American in 1961 by industrialist Egidi Cressi.

The top of the statue is in 10 feet of water and can be seen easily from the surface. The base rests on a sandy bottom, 20 feet down, and is surrounded by huge brain corals and elkhorn formations. Stingrays and barracuda inhabit the site. A buoy marks the statue's location, but still it is difficult to pinpoint. If you are unfamiliar with navigating in the park, join one of the commercial dive trips. Extreme shallows in the area make running aground a threat.

More easily found is **Molasses Reef,** marked by a huge, lighted steel tower in the southeast corner of the park. It is the area's most popular reef dive. Named after a ship carrying molasses that ran aground here, the reef actually provides several dives, depending on where your boat is moored. Moorings M21 through M23 are for diving. M1 through M20 are shallow and better for snorkeling. High profile, coral ridges form the perimeter of a series of coral ridges, grooves, overhangs, ledges and swim-through tunnels. In one area, divers see huge silver tarpon, walls of grunts, snappers, squirrel fish and Spanish hogfish. In another, divers swim over an ancient Spanish anchor. Visibility is often more than 100 ft, but divers should check the current at Molasses before entering the water since an occasional strong flow makes the area undiveable. Depths vary from very shallow to approximately 40 ft.

Slightly northeast of Molasses is **French Reef**, an area many consider the prettiest in the park. Swim-through tunnels, caves, and ledges typify the site. Coral mounds are carpeted with sea fans, basket and tube sponges, soft corals, and anemones. Depths are shallow to 45 ft.

To the north of French is the wreck of the *Benwood*, a World War II freighter that was hit by a German submarine. Sunk as a navigational hazard by the Coast Guard, she now sits on a sandy bottom in 45 ft of water.

The 300-ft wreck is a favorite night dive as well as a good site for photography and fish watching during the day. Lobsters, huge morays and sting rays hide in the sand beneath the wreck. Huge parrotfish and grouper are frequently sighted here.

Carysfort Reef, located in the northeast corner of the park, is the least populated dive site. A long boat ride keeps this area from becoming a regular spot for the dive operators. The fish population is huge and offers some real entertainment for video and still photographers. We discovered some dramatic overhangs the hard way—by surfacing without first looking up. One resident barracuda enjoys swimming up face-to-face with divers in hope of a hand out. He is hard to ignore, but feeding fish is discouraged so resist the urge to tote lunch. Displays of staghorn, elkhorn and star coral formations line the walls of the reef with depths varying from very shallow to 65 ft. A good dive for novice and experienced divers.

Just south of Carysfort Reef is **The Elbow**, where you'll view the twisted remains of a wooden Civil War wreck, and two steamers, The *City of Washington*, and The *Tonawanda*. Depths average 40 feet. Visibility is usually good with an occasional strong current.

KEY LARGO'S ARTIFICIAL REEF

In November, 1987, two vintage Coast Guard cutters were sunk off Key Largo by a team of Navy divers.

The 1930's-era sister cutters *Bibb* and *Duane* whose careers took them from the Caribbean and Cap Cod and included duties in the North Atlantic, Pacific and Mediterranean, were towed to their final resting site following cleaning and removal of potential hazards for divers.

The *Bibb* sits on her side in 125 ft. of water while the *Duane* sits upright at 130 ft. The top of the *Duane* can be viewed at 75 ft. They rest seven miles offshore and one mile south of Molasses Reef. This area is a buffer zone around the Key Largo National Marine Sanctuary. Both ships have attracted huge grouper, schooling tropicals, barracuda, eels and rays. An occasional hammerhead or nurse shark makes an appearance.

The ships, now camouflaged with a thin layer of coral, were part of a seven vessel "Secretary" class built by the Coast Guard in the late 1930s, with their original role as long-range rescue ships, according to Dr. Robert Scheina, a Coast Guard historian. "The vessels were also built to prevent poaching by Japanese fishing vessels in Alaskan Waters and a third purpose—one quite familiar to today's Coast Guard. There was a problem with opium smuggling from the Orient to various outlets on the west coast of the United States. The vessels were utilized for drug interdiction back then."

With spare parts for the *Bibb* and *Duane* difficult to obtain and with excessive maintenance costs the Coast Guard de-commissioned the ships in 1985 and turned them over to the United States Maritime Administration for disposal.

South of Pennekamp Park lies **Pickles Reef**, a shallow area rich with marine life, sea fans and boulder corals. Near Pickles is **Conch Reef**, a wall dive which drops off to more than 100 feet, and the wreck of the *Eagle*, a 287-foot freighter, sunk intentionally to create an artificial reef. Residents of the wreck include parrot fish, schools of grunt, sargeant majors, moray eels and angels.

Another popular site frequented by Islamorada dive shops is **Alligator Reef**, home to walls of grunts, parrotfish and groupers and an occasional nurse shark. There are some nice stands of elkhorn and brain corals. More spectacular though are the reefs surrounding the

Marquesas Islands, 30 miles from Key West and the Dry Tortugas, 70 miles off Key West.

DIVING THE MIDDLE KEYS

The Marathon area from Conch Key to the Seven Mile Bridge is thought of as the Middle Keys. Here the dive sites are a bit less crowded than Key Largo and in some respects offer more variety. When currents are mild you can dive the old bridges which abound with fish, sponges and soft corals. Sombrero Reef is the most popular diving area off Marathon. Good visibility and a wide range of depths make this spot a favorite for novice and experienced divers. A maze of coral canyons provide endless entertainment for fish watching and photography. Depths range from shallow to 40 feet. A huge tower makes Sombrero easy to find. Boaters must tie up to the mooring bouys on the reef.

Just slightly to the north of Sombrero lies the wreck of the **Thunderbolt**, upright in 110 feet of water. The 188-foot wreck is covered with a dense carpet of soft corals and alive with a bustling fish population. Here you'll spot numerous barracuda, sargeant majors, queen and grey angels, blue tangs and eels. Coffins patch, just north of the Thunderbolt wreck, is a shallow reef with an average 20- to 30-ft depth. The reef is formed by mounds of pillar coral intermixed with thickets of elkhorn and brain coral.

DIVING THE LOWER KEYS AND KEY WEST

Looe Key National Marine Sanctuary, is named for a British frigate, the **HMS Looe**, which ran aground in the 1700's. It is the favorite dive site of the Lower Keys. Shallow depths, to 35 feet, draw you through a garden of elkhorn and staghorn corals inhabited by Cuban hogfish, queen parrotfish, huge barracuda, and longsnout butterfly fish. Shallow areas are dominated by seagrasses and coral rubble where a calm environment provides habitat for many plants and animals.

Diving off Key West includes tours of Cotrell Key, Sand Key and the Western Dry Marks. Sand Key ranges from the surface down to 45 ft. A light house makes it an easy find for boaters. Cosgrove Reef is gaining in popularity with Key West divers too. Here large heads of boulder and brain coral intermix with soft corals. Huge pelagic fish and graceful rays lure divers to this area.

Wreck of the Duane

Advanced divers may want to tour the ***Cayman Salvage Master***, at 90 feet. This 180-ft. vessel was purposely sunk to form an artificial reef.

Seldom visited, though pristine for diving, are the Marquesa Islands, 30 miles off Key West. Extreme shallows both enroute and surrounding the islands make the boat trip difficult in all but the calmest seas and docking impossible for all but shallow draft cats and trimarans. Check with Lost Reef Adventures (305-296-9737) for trip availability.

Seventy miles to the west are the Dry Tortugas where the most fabulous diving in the Keys can be found. No services though. You reach the area by charter boat or seaplane (305-294- 6978), and should carry in all of your gear and air. Check with Key West dive shops for the availability of trips (see also Aerial Tours chapter). For the very adventurous, overnight camping trips can be arranged.

DIVE OPERATORS

The following operators provide guided reef and wreck trips. Many also can arrange complete dive and accommodation packages.

KEY LARGO

Admiral Dive
MM 103.2
Key Largo FL 33037
800-346-DIVE or 305-451-1114

Amy Slate's Amoray Dive Center, Inc.
104250 Overseas Highway
MM104
Key Largo, FL 33037
800-426-6729 or 800-4-A-MORAY

Aqua-Nuts
103750 Overseas Hwy
Key Largo FL 33037

Atlantis Dive Center, Inc.
51 Garden Cove Dr.
MM 106.5
Key Largo FL 33037
800-331-DIVE or 305-451-3020

Captain Corky's Diver's World
MM 99.5
Key Largo FL 33037
800-445-8231 or 305-451-3200

Captain Slate's Atlantis Dive Center, Inc.
51 Garden Cove Drive
Key Largo FL 33037
800-331-3483 or 305-451-3020

Coral Reef Park Co.
P.O. Box 1560
Key Largo FL 33037
800-344-8175 or 305-451-1621

Divers Den of Key Largo
110 Ocean Dr., MM 100
Key Largo, FL 33037
800-527-DIVE or 305-451-DIVE

Stephen Frink Photographic
MM 102.5
Key Largo, FL 33037
800-451-3737 or 305-451-3737

Harry Keitz American Diving Headquarters
MM 105.5
P.O. Box 1250
Key Largo FL 33037
800-634-8464 or 305-451-0037

Inc.
MM 105.5
Key Largo FL

Island Ventures
MM 103.9
Key Largo FL 33037
305-451-4957

Keys Diver
MM 100
Key Largo FL
305-451-1177

Ocean Divers, Inc
522 Caribbean Dr.
Key Largo FL 33037
800-451-1113 or 305-451-1113

Pennekamp State Park Dive Center
Located at John Pennekamp Park
800-272-4148 or 305-451-6322

Quiescence Diving Service
MM103.5
Key Largo FL 33037
305-451-2440

Sea Dwellers Sports Center
99850 Overseas Hwy,
MM 100
Key Largo FL 33037
800-451-3540 or 305-451-3640

Silent World Dive Center, Inc.
P.O. Box 2363, MM 103.2
Key Largo FL 33037
800-966-DIVE or 305-451-3252

Conch Republic Divers, Inc.
90311 Overseas Highway
Tavernier FL 33070
800-274-DIVE or 305-852-1655

Florida Keys Dive Center
90500 Overseas Hwy,
MM 90.5
Plantation Key, FL 33070

Tavernier Dive Center
MM 90.5
Tavernier FL 33070
800-537-3253 or 305-852-4007

ISLAMORADA

Bud 'n Mary's Dive Center
MM 80
Islamorada FL 33036
800-344-7352 or 305-664-2211

Cheeca Divers at Cheeca Lodge
MM 82
Islamorada FL 33036
800-934-8377 or 305-664-2777

Holiday Isle Dive Shop
P.O. Box 482
Islamorada, FL 33036
800-327-7070 or 305-664-4145

Lady Cyana Divers
MM 85.9
Islamorada FL 33036
800-221-8717 or 305-664-8717

Ocean Quest Dive Center
87000 Overseas Hwy, MM 87
Islamorada FL 33036
800-356-8798 or 305-852-8770

Reef Shop Dive Center
84771 Overseas Hwy., MM 84.7
Islamorada FL 33036
305-664-4385

Treasure Divers, Inc.
85500 Overseas Hwy, MM 85.5
Islamorada FL 33036
800-356-9887 or 305-664-5111

World Down Under
MM 81.5
Islamorada FL 33036
305-664-9312, FL 800-245-DIVE

MARATHON

Abyss Pro Dive Center
13175 Overseas Highway
Marathon FL 33050
800-457-0134 or 305-743-2126

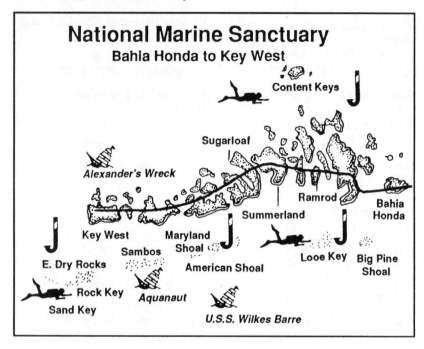

National Marine Sanctuary
Bahia Honda to Key West

Content Keys

Sugarloaf

Alexander's Wreck

Ramrod

Bahia Honda

Summerland

Key West   Maryland Shoal

Sambos   American Shoal   Looe Key   Big Pine Shoal

E. Dry Rocks

Rock Key   Aquanaut

Sand Key

U.S.S. Wilkes Barre

Hall's Diving Center
1994 Overseas Hwy

Marathon FL 33050

800-331-HALL or 305-743-5929

Hurricane Aqua-Center
10800 Overseas Hwy
Marathon FL 33050
305-743-2400

Marathon Divers
MM 53.5
Marathon FL 33050
305-289-1141

Middle Keys Scuba Center
MM 53

Marathon FL 33050
305-743-2902

Ocean Adventures
Hawk's Cay Marina
MM 61
Marathon FL 33050
800-432-2242 or 305-743-9000

Ocean Equipment
2250 Overseas Hwy
Marathon FL 33050
305-743-4644

Tilden's Pro Dive Shop
MM 49.5
Marathon FL 33050
800-223-4563 or 305-743-5422

BIG PINE & THE LOWER KEYS

Cudjoe Gardens Dive Center
802 Drost Drive
Cudjoe Key FL 33042
305-745-2357

Looe Key Dive Center
P.O. Box 509
MM 27.5
Ramrod Key FL 33042
800-942-KEYS or 305-872-2215

Reef Runner Dive Shop
MM 25
Summerland Key FL 33042
305-745-1549

Inner space Dive Shop
MM 29.5
Big Pine Key FL 33043
800-538-2896 or 305-872-2319

Underseas, Inc.
MM 30.5
Big Pine Key FL 33043
800-446-5663 or 305-872-9555

KEY WEST

Stars & Stripes
703 Duval St.
Key West FL 33040
305-296-8986

Captain's Corner Dive Center
Ocean Key House Hotel
0 Duval Street
Key West FL 33040
305-296-8865; 800-328-9815

Dive Sanctuary
1221 Duvall St.
Key West FL 33040
305-294-2772

Key West Divers, Inc.
U.S. 1 Stock Island
Key West FL 33040
305-294-7177, 800-87-DIVER

Key West Pro Dive Shop, Inc.
1605 Roosevelt Blvd.
Key West, FL 33040
305-296-3823; 800-426-0707

Key West Pro Dive Shop
3128 N. Roosevelt
Key West FL 33040
800-426-0707 or 305-296-3823

Looker Key West Diving Excellence
P.O. Box 4035
Key West FL 33041
800-245-2249 or 305-294-2249

Lost Reef Adventures
261 Margaret St.
At Lands End Village
Key West FL 33040
800-633-6833 or 305-296-9737

Promethean Adventures Charters
1221 Duval St.
Key West FL 33040
305-294-2772

Reef Raiders Dive Shop
109 Duval St.
Key West FL 33040
800-741-0660 or 305-294-0442

Reef Runner Dive Shop
MM 25
Summerland Key FL 33042
305-745-1549

Sea Center Dive Shop
MM 29.5
Big Pine Key FL 33043
305-872-2319

Underseas, Inc.
MM 30.5
Big Pine Key FL 33043
305-872-9555; 800-446-5663

KEY WEST

Adventures and Treasure
703 Duval St.
Key West FL 33040
305-296-8986

Captain's Corner Dive Center
Ocean Key House Hotel
0 Duval Street
Key West FL 33040
305-296-8865

Key West Divers, Inc.
U.S. 1 Stock Island
Key West FL 33040
305-294-7177; 800-87-DIVER

Key West Pro Dive Shop, Inc.
1605 Roosevelt Blvd.
Key West FL 33040
305-296-3823; 800-426-0707

Lost Reef Adventures
261 Margaret St.
At Lands End Village
Key West FL 33040
305-296-9737; 800-633-6833

Nautical Excursions
528 A Front St.
Key West FL 33040
305-294-2911; 305-294-3119

Omega Blue
P.O. Box 6421
Key West FL 33040
305-296-2386

Promethean Adventures Charters
1221 Duval St.
Key West FL 33040
305-294-2772

Reef Raiders Dive Shop
109 Duval St.
Key West FL 33040
305-294-0442

SNORKELING

If you can swim, you'll love snorkeling. Florida Keys offshore reefs offer endless entertainment to anyone who can peer through a mask. There are shallow shipwrecks, such as the wreck of the *San Pedro*, an underwater archaeological preserve off Islamorada, miles of coral canyons and pinnacles, the famous Statue of Christ in Key Largo, and every imaginable fish along the entire coast. The best spots to snorkel are the outer reefs. Morning and afternoon boat trips are widely available. If given a choice, select the morning trips which are less crowded with usually calmer wind and seas.

Take a snorkeling lesson if you're new to the sport. A short pool demonstration will allow you to get comfortable using the gear before you try it in the ocean. Many hotels and dive shops offer classes.

If high winds or storms cancel ocean tours, you can still explore the bays or oceanside lagoons (dive shops will rent you the gear). We found a number of juvenile barracuda, parrot fish, filefish, angels and grunts around the bayside hotel docks and swimming lagoons. Just off the beach at John Pennekamp State Park are some old cannons and a sunken car. This artificial reef attracts numerous fish and crustaceans. An occasional manatee has been spotted there too.

For a fee, you can snorkel over the first underwater hotel—Jules' Undersea Lodge located in the Key Largo Undersea Park. The park is a protected lagoon and open 365 days a year. Though the fish and visibility do not rival the offshore reefs this is a good spot for beginners or when storms rule out ocean tours. To reach the lagoon turn toward the ocean at the "Undersea Park" sign (MM 103.2). The lagoon is at the end of the road.

Places to Avoid

Snorkeling is unsafe in the brackish and fresh waters of the Everglades—home to alligators. There is a crocodile sanctuary on the northernmost tip of Key Largo which must be avoided. Alligators and, even more so, crocodiles are unpredictable and despite a sluggish appearance must be considered extremely dangerous to humans.

EQUIPMENT

Snorkeling tours include use of a mask, snorkel and inflatable safety vest. Swim fins are almost always part of the deal and are an added benefit. They make swimming much easier and will help you keep pace with the parade of fish you'll be joining. If you plan on a lot of snorkeling, by all means purchase your own equipment. A proper-fitting mask and a comfortable snorkel make the experience much more rewarding. Masks and snorkels are made from rubber or silicone. The silicone is more expensive, but softer against the skin and somewhat more comfortable for prolonged use. Don't mix. Oils in rubber will badly discolor silicone. If you wear eyeglasses you may want to invest in an optically-corrected mask before your trip. They start at about $95 US and can be ordered from most dive shops. You can wear contacts with a standard mask, but run the risk of losing them underwater.

Expect difficulty sealing your mask if you sport a beard or mustache. Water tends to wick in along the hairs. Try a bit of vaseline around the rim of your mask. It may reduce or eliminate the problem. Shaving is the most reliable solution.

Long hair should be brushed back, away from your face, before putting on a mask. One thin hair becomes a very efficient siphon of water. Check for a good fit by placing the mask against your face (sans straps) and inhale. If you can't easily shake the mask off, the fit is good.

NEVER USE EAR PLUGS OR SWIMMING GOGGLES FOR SNORKELING. Pressure from even a very shallow dive can cause mask squeeze. Your nose must be included in the mask to allow you to exhale slightly and equalize the pressure as you descend. Use of ear plugs underwater can cause serious and permanent damage to your eardrums.

Before boarding the snorkel-tour boat, be sure to pick up a container of anti-fogging solution. Available in most dive shops, it will keep the glass part of your mask crystal clear. Without it your mask will quickly fog up. In a pinch, if anti-fog solution is unavailable, rub a bit of saliva around the inside of the glass and rinse lightly.

During winter the water temperature drops from 85 ° down to 70-75 °F. Some wetwear is desirable. A shorty wetsuit or a lycra wetskin will protect you from the sun and keep you warm. Wetskins are the most popular with snorkelers as they are easier to put on than wetsuits and cost a lot less. They will protect you from sunburn too—often the biggest problem a snorkeler encounters. While snorkeling, a thin layer of water over your back keeps you feeling deceptively cool, but does nothing to block out the harmful rays of the sun. Be safe. If you don't have a wetskin or light wetsuit, wear a long-sleeved shirt and consider long pants if you are fair-skinned.

Look, But Don't Touch

Everything living is protected in Florida's marine parks. Wearing gloves, touching corals and feeding fish are prohibited. Spearfishing is outlawed. Certain foods eaten by humans can be unhealthy and often fatal to fish. Touching corals may kill them or cause infection or disease which can spread to surrounding corals. Touching any corals may cause an allergic reaction, but touching fire coral will give you a painful sting.

It is best to familiarize yourself with the marine life before you visit the reefs. Fish and coral identification books and submersible sheets can be picked up at dive shops.

Avoid wearing dangling jewelry. To a normally harmless, but somewhat toothy barracuda it may offer the same appeal as a fishing lure.

Display a diver-down flag any time you are in the water.

SNORKELING TOURS

Half-day tours to the underwater sanctuaries lead in popularity, but if you are after adventure you'll find numerous sail-snorkel trips which visit remote islands, and shoals. New, designed-for-snorkeling, shallow-draft trimarans and catamarans visit out-islands and shallow reefs. Seaplane fly-in excursions to the Dry Tortugas, a magnificent chain of remote, uninhabited, coral-fringed islands, leave from Key West.

If your traveling with scuba-equipped companions, you'll find most dive boats allow you to join the tour for a reduced fee. Stop in at any

dive shop for trip schedules. But the best trips are aboard the snorkel boats. They park on the shallow reefs and usually visit more than one site. Or you can spend a week aboard one of the live-aboard sailing yachts and tour the entire area. Physical fitness buffs may wish to combine paddling with snorkeling tours. Both Key West Kayak and Mosquito Coast make that offer (see Canoe Tours chapter for listings).

Half-day snorkeling tours average $25 with some as high as $50. Camera and video rentals or use of special gear are extra.

Biscayne National Park

Biscayne National Park is the largest marine park in the United States, consisting of 181,500 acres of islands, bays and offshore coral reefs.

Snorkeling excursions are offered aboard a 53-ft., glass-bottom motor yacht, *Reef Rover IV* by Biscayne National Underwater Park, Inc., P.O. Box 1270, Homestead, FL 33030. Phone: 305-247-2400.

Key Largo

Southeast of the Florida Peninsula, where the Keys begin their extension into the Gulf of Mexico, lies one of nature's oldest and most artfully crafted underwater gardens, the Key Largo National Marine Sanctuary. It is located in the Atlantic Ocean beginning three miles seaward of Key Largo and extends out to 300-ft. depths, some eight miles at sea on the continental shelf. Designated a National Marine Sanctuary in 1975, it encompasses 100 square miles of submerged coral reefs. Over one million divers and snorkelers visit the sanctuary each year.

Snorkeling trips to the reef can be booked at almost any dive shop. Try Coral Reef Park Co., MM 102.5 (inside John Pennekamp State Park, 305-451-1621), MM 103.4 or the Sun Diver Station Snorkel Shack, oceanside, (451-2220) at the Holiday Inn docks, MM 103. A snorkeling-sailing trimaran tour can be booked at John Pennekamp State Park, MM 102.5 (451-1621). Snorkel tours leave the park docks at 9:00 am, noon and 3:00 pm.

The Keys Diver at MM 100, oceanside, has a new 40-ft. boat designed especially for snorkeling. Family and group rates available. Phone: 305-451-1177.

Finz Photo and Dive Center at MM 100 (across from Holiday Inn) offers snorkel-with-the-dolphins tours, video shoots and photo shoots. Underwater video and photo rentals available.

Admiral Dive Center at MM 103.2 takes snorkelers aboard the 65-ft. *Admiral I* to Pennekamp Reefs. Cameras and gear rentals available. Phone: 305-451-1114.

Harry Keitz's **American Diving Headquarters, Inc.** at MM 105.5 has been serving the area since 1962. Phone: 305-451-0037, 451-0039.

Captain Corky's Divers' World is at MM 99.5. Custom snorkeling charters, including three- and five-day live-aboard trips are offered. Phone: 451-3200. Write to P.O. Box 1663, Key Largo, FL 33037.

Combine a luxury cruising and snorkeling excursion to the marine park aboard *Witts End*, a 51-ft. ketch. Phone: 305-451-3354. Docked behind Marina Del Mar, MM 100. Live-aboard trips are also offered.

For additional information write to Captains Witt, P.O. Box 625, Key Largo, FL 33037.

ISLAMORADA

Offshore on the Atlantic side you can explore the wreckage of the 287-ton Dutch ship, *San Pedro*, one of Florida's oldest artificial reefs. Remains of the ship rest in a sand pocket 18 feet below the surface. The visibility is not as good as the offshore reefs, but it is an interesting dive nonetheless. A host of sea creatures live amidst the ballast stones and coral heads next to the wreck, including gobies, damsels, moray eels and groupers.

The ship was carrying 16,000 pesos in Mexican silver and numerous crates of Chinese porcelain when she wrecked in 1733.

Contact the Long Key State Park office at 305-664-4815 for tours to the wreck. Boaters use LORAN coordinates 14082.1, 43320.6. The wreck is approximately one and one-quarter nautical miles south from Indian Key. Be sure to tie up to the mooring buoys to prevent anchor damage to the site.

Islamorada dive shops visit Molasses, Alligator and Tennessee reefs—all named for a ship wrecked at the site. The reefs range in depth fromshallow to about 40 feet. Snorkeling trips are offered at the Holiday Isle Dive Center, MM 84.9. Phone: 305-664-4145.

Daily reef and wreck tours are also offered at Bud n' Mary's Dive Center, MM 79.8 (Phone: 305-664-2211) and World Down Under, MM 81.5. Phone: 305-664-9312.

Marathon - Big Pine Key

Sombrero Reef and Looe Key National Marine Sanctuary both offer superb reef snorkeling. Depths range from two to 35 feet.

Marathon Divers, MM 54, has daily reef trips. Phone: 305-289-1141. In Big Pine Key book a tour with Underseas Inc. at MM 30.5. Phone: 305-872-2700.

Excursions to the island where PT 109 was filmed can be arranged through Strike Zone Charters. On the four and one-half hour trip, owners Mary & Larry Threlkeld include snorkeling gear and a fish fry on the beach. Phone: 800-654-9560 or 305-872-9863. Write to

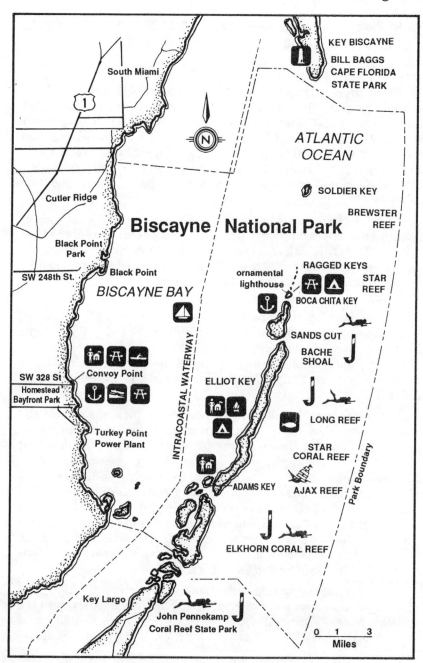

Strike Zone Charters, Dolphin Marina, MM 28.5, Rt. 1, Box 610 D, Big Pine Key, FL 33043.

Key West

Key West offers perhaps the most diversified collection of adventure-snorkeling cruises in the islands. Sail-snorkel cruises visit secluded islands surrounded with beautiful coral reefs, often including lunch and refreshments. Catered gourmet meals and even snorkeling weddings for those who find romance at sea are offered by Key West Yacht Excursions. They claim their vessels are perfect for "tying the knoticals." More usually, guests settle for the picnic lunch. Phone: 305-296-2797.

Captain Ron Canning is personal friends with several local pods of dolphins and offers dolphin-watch, snorkeling excursions aboard the luxury catamaran, *Patty C* . Phone: 305-294-6306. Prior reservations a must. On neighboring Stock Island, personalized charters can be arranged aboard the six-passenger trimaran, *Fantasea*. Phone: 305-296-0362.

History buffs will want to book a snorkel trip on the 74-ft. schooner, *Wolf*. Stop by the dock at the foot of William St., Key West Bight Marina. Phone: 305-296-9653 (WOLF). Small groups—up to six—are given an unforgettable adventure aboard the 42-ft. schooner *Island Belle*. Half-day reef trips depart at 9:30 am and 1:30 pm. Phone: 305-292-1345.

Sail-racing fans will delight in touring the out-islands aboard the *Stars & Stripes*, a huge 54-ft., 49-passenger replica of the racing catamaran famed by Dennis Conner. This ninth version was designed especially for cruising the shallow channels and reefs of Key West. For maximum comfort and enjoyment, this sailing yacht features a 29-ft. beam, glass bottom viewing, and a fully shaded lounge. The ultra shallow draft (25") allows the captain to pull up to sandy beaches at Woman Key and other spots which are off limits to many charter boats. See the *Stars & Stripes* at Land's End Marina. You can book a tour at Lost Reef Adventures, 261 Margaret Street, Key West. Phone: 305-294-7877 or 305 294-PURR.

Two more fabulous catamarans, the 60-ft. *Fury* and 50-ft. *Sebago* offer sail-snorkel tours out of Key West. The Fury departs from the Truman Annex (West end of Greene St.) at 9:30 am and 1:00 pm; it visits Sand Key, Rock Key, Eastern Dry Rocks and Western Sambo—

all coral reef out-islands. Phone: 294-8899. The *Sabago* has a sales booths at various sites on Duval St and one in the Hoggs' Breath Restaurant parking lot. Phone: 305-294-5687. Trips include equipment and soft drinks.

Dry Tortugas

The Dry Tortugas, 70 miles off Key West, are surrounded by pristine coral reefs and wrecks. The shallows can be explored in two to four feet of water though you are less apt to suffer coral scrapes in somewhat deeper water. These uninhabited islands can be reached by boat or seaplane. The Marquesas, equally magnificent in reef life, are approachable only in periods of exceptionally calm seas. Boating information is available though the U.S. Coast Guard.

Underwater film maker and adventurer, Tom Jackson offers specialized tours to local shallow wrecks and on calm days to the Dry Tortugas or the Marquesas. On the 30-mile crossing to the Marquesas you can spot sharks and rays as they dart under the boat along the sandy bottom. Armies of tulip shells with resident hermit crabs guard the remote island beaches. Tom is an expert on local marine life and known for his work on the James Bond thriller, "License to Kill" and Goldie Hawn's movie, "Criss Cross". Trips are aboard the *Happy Hour*, a 17-ft. Boston whaler or *Magic Hour*, a 21-ft. power boat., Sign up at Lost Reef Adventures, 261 Margaret Street. Phone: 305-296-9737 or 305-294-7280.

Seaplane-snorkel tours to the Dry Tortugas can be booked Key West Seaplane, Junior College Rd. Phone: 305-294-6978.

Chalk's Airlines offers fly-snorkel tours to Fort Jefferson aboard their flying boats. Phone: 800-424-2557.

Boaters

Be sure to display a divers flag if you are snorkeling from your own boat. Strong currents may be encountered on the outside reefs. Check before disembarking. One person should always remain on board. Be aware of weather, sea conditions and your own limitations before going offshore. Sudden storms, waterspouts and weather-related, fast moving fronts are not uncommon. Nautical charts are available at marinas and boating supply outlets throughout the Keys.

At the Key Largo and Looe Key National Marine Sanctuaries there are mooring buoys to which you can attach your boat, so that you do not have to drop anchor. If no bouys are available, you should drop anchor only in sandy areas. The bottom in sandy areas appears white.

In protected areas of the Keys, destruction of coral formations through grounding or imprudent anchoring can lead to penalties and fines of up to $50,000. Minor damage to coral fines start at $150.

Give yourself plenty of room to maneuver. For Key Largo National Marine Sanctuary use chart 11451 or 11462, and for Looe Key National Marine Sanctuary use chart 11442 or 11445.

SWIM WITH THE DOLPHINS

If you are fascinated by dolphins, a unique and unusual encounter awaits you in any one of three Florida Keys facilities—a chance to swim freely with the gentle animals. No longer do you have to sit back and watch the beautiful creatures jump through hoops; now you can swim in their pool and join in their playful stunts.

You must be at least 13 years old, know how to swim and attend an orientation session with a dolphin trainer. Life jackets available. Advance reservations are a must.

The in-water sessions are 30 minutes. A trainer is in charge at all times, yet once you are comfortable in the water you are encouraged to be creative and very active, to interact by diving down with mask and snorkel.

When you first enter the water the dolphins will "turn on" their sonar and check you over. You will hear a clicking, whistling sound. Once their get-acquainted ritual is complete they may present a chin to be scratched or kissed. When they roll to one side showing their dorsal fins, it's a way of telling guests to grab hold and take an exciting ride through the water.

Don't be alarmed if one comes charging straight at you with lightening-speed. They like to play "chicken" and will veer off to one side at the last moment. Of course, no one can ever predict entirely how an animal taken from the wild will behave, but these individuals are carefully screened for gentle character and the right personality.

"Our dolphins really enjoy contact with people," says Mandy Rodriguez, director of the Dolphin Research Center. "Actually, they (the dolphins) think we are providing people for their fun and enjoyment."

Located on Grassy Key near Marathon, the Dolphin Research Center maintains liaisons with university research programs and independent investigators around the world. A not-for-profit teaching and research facility, the center has received national attention when called upon to accept sick or wounded dolphins found in coastal waters.

The center also accepts dolphins from other marine research facilities at which the animals sometimes suffer from overcrowded conditions. Still more dolphins, "burnt out" from years of performing in aquariums, spend their "retirement" at the center and achieve a complete rejuvenation living in the warm waters of the Atlantic instead of a tank.

Islamorada-based Theater of the Sea offers swim programs three times a day, along with continuous marine shows featuring sea lions, sharks and other marine species. As part of the dolphin program, trainer Gina Gouvan has developed special exercises for spinal-cord-injured patients. Interaction with the dolphins has been useful in easing depression and in community re-integration. The patients must be alert.

At Dolphins Plus on Key Largo, visitors enjoy much more than a dolphin swim. A special orientation program offers an hour-long pre-swim seminar about the endangered marine species.

There are additional field trips and dolphin-research programs offered. For more information contact the dolphin facilities. Cost for the swim programs starts at $60.

Theatre of the Sea, MM 84, Islamorada FL 33036. Phone: 305-664-2431.

Dolphin Research Center, MM 59, Grassy Key, Marathon FL 33050. Phone: 305-289-1121.

Dolphins Plus Inc., 147 Corrine Place, Key Largo 33037. Phone: 305-451-1993.

SECTION III

ATTRACTIONS

EVERGLADES
Everglades City

Eden of the Everglades, on Route 29 two miles south of Hwy 41, offers boat tours, a unique wetlands zoo and scenic boat tours through wildlife habitats. Boats depart hourly starting at 11 am. Turn right before Everglades City Bridge. Phone: 1-800-543-3367.

Jungle Erv's Everglades Information Station on Route 29 in Everglades City features an alligator zoo, exotic birds and a petting zoo. Phone: 813-695-2805.

Tamiami Trail

Wooten's Air Boat Tours and Swamp Buggy Rides, on U.S. 41 two miles west of Ochopee, displays hundreds of alligators and live snakes. Everglades wilderness tours by airboat or swamp buggy depart every half-hour. Phone: 813-695-2781.

The Miccosukee Indian Village, MM 70, 25 miles west of Miami on the Tamiami Trail (U.S. 41) is open daily, year round. Miccosukee craftsmen demonstrate woodcraft, doll making, basket weaving and intricate patchwork sewing. Lively alligator wrestling and airboat rides highlight the village activities. A museum features tribal films and artifacts. Phone: 305-223-8388 or 305-223-8380. Write to P.O. Box 440021, Miami FL 33144.

MIAMI AREA

The Monkey Jungle, just off U.S. 1 in South Dade, is home to nearly 500 primates, most running free on a 20-acre reserve. It is one of the few protected habitats for endangered primates in the United States and the only one that the general public can explore. You are caged and the monkeys run wild. To get to the park, take the Florida Turnpike's Homestead Extension (Hwy 821) south to the Cutler Ridge Blvd/S.W. 216 St. exit, get onto 216 St. westbound, then go west for 5 miles; or take U.S. 1 south to S.W. 216 St. then go west on 216 for 3 1/2 miles. Phone: 305-235-1611. Write 14805 S.W. 216 St. Miami FL 33170.

Miami Metrozoo is open every day from 10 am to 5:30 pm. There are more than 2,800 magnificent wild animals living in a cageless natural environment; Paws, a new children's petting zoo; the Zoofari Monorail which takes you on an air-conditioned safari; elephant rides, koalas, flamingos, white tigers and a 1 1/2-acre tropical aviary. Admission is $6.50 for adults, $3.50 for children. Ticket booth closes at 4 pm. Metrozoo is about 20 minutes from Miami International Airport. From U.S. 1, take S.W. 152nd St. exit west three miles to the entrance. From the Turnpike Extension, take the S.W. 152nd St. exit west a quarter-mile to the Metrozoo entrance. Phone: 305-251-0403.

Miami Seaquarium is south Florida's largest marine attraction. Seals, sharks, dolphins and killer whales are the stars. Continuous shows. Magnificent aquariums. Phone: 305-361-5705. Located at 4400 Rickenbacker Causeway, Miami FL 33156.

Parrot Jungle and Gardens, south of Miami International Airport off U.S. 1, offers encounters with talking birds, walks through beautiful tropical gardens, trained-bird shows in the "Parrot Bowl", where macaws and cockatoos perform feats which defy the imagination. Besides the 1,100 parrots there are huge alligators, giant tortoises, peacocks, exotic plants and a petting zoo. Fun for all ages. Open from 9:30 am to 6 pm. Adults $9.75; children $4.00. Wheelchairs and strollers available. Phone: 305-666-7834. Located at 11000 S.W. 57th Avenue, Miami FL 33156.

Alligator Wrestling

Orchid Jungle features orchids from every part of the world. Located at 26715 S.W. 157th Avenue, Miami FL 33031. Phone: 1-800-327-2832; FL 1-800-344-2457 or 305-247-4824.

Weeks Air Museum displays more than 30 vintage aircraft, engines and propellers. Phone: 305-233-5197. Located at 14710 S.W. 128 Street, Miami FL 33186.

FLORIDA KEYS

The *African Queen*, famed by Humphrey Bogart and Katharine Hepburn, is enthroned at the Holiday Inn docks, MM 100. Half-hour cruises on the *Queen* may be booked at the Holiday Inn gift shop. Phone: 305-451-4655.

Theater of the Sea, MM 84.5, Islamorada, is the world's second oldest marine park, established in 1946 utilizing the excavations of the old Flagler railroad. The resulting main lagoon is a huge, treelined and natural ecosystem. Visitors can shake hands with or be kissed by a sea lion, touch a shark or stroke a turtle, feed a stingray or pet a dolphin. There are continuous shows from 9:30 to 4 pm. Phone 305-664-2431 or write P.O. Box 407, Islamorada FL 33036.

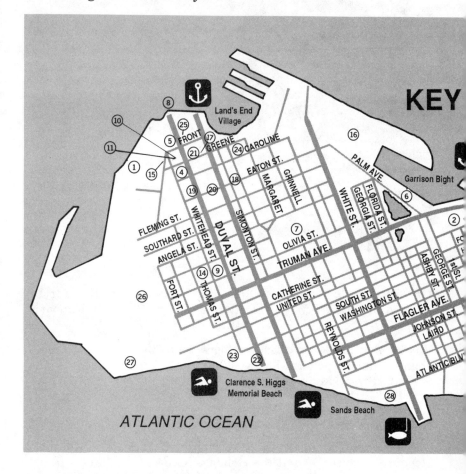

Key West Attractions and Points of Interest

1. Mallory Square
2. Trolley Barn
3. Welcome Center
4. Audubon House
5. Chamber of Commerce
6. Charter Boats
7. Cemetery; Maine Monument
8. Glass Bottom Boat
9. Hemingway House
10. Key West Aquarium
11. Conch Train
12. Key West Golf Course
13. Key West Seaplane Base
14. Lighthouse Museum
15. Mel Fisher's
    Treasure Museum

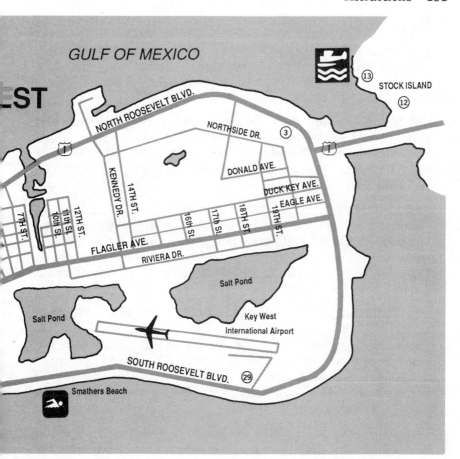

16. Navy Base
17. Old City Hall
18. Old Stone
    Methodist Church
19. Oldest House
20. Saint Paul's
    Episcopal Church
21. Sloppy Joe's

22. Southernmost House
23. Southernmost Point
24. Turtle Kraals
25. Waterfront Playhouse
26. Truman Annex
27. Fort Zachary State Park
28. West Martello Tower
29. E. Martello Tower

Key West

The Conch Tour Train is a 90-minute, narrated tour of Key West. It is the fastest way to familiarize yourself with the entire city. Board the train at 601 Duval Street, Key West FL 33040. Phone: 305-294-5161.

Old Town Trolley Tours make 12 stops for sightseeing and shopping in Key West. Passengers may disembark for lunch and rejoin the tour later. Tours begin every 30 minutes. The station is at 1910 North Roosevelt Blvd, Key West FL 33040. Phone 305-296-6688.

Audubon House and Gardens display 18th- and 19th-century Audubon engravings and a gallery of porcelain bird sculptures. Formerly the home of Captain John H. Geiger, the house was restored as a museum to commemorate John James Audubon's 1832 visit to Key West. At 205 Whitehead Street, Key West FL 33040. Phone 305-294-2116.

Mel Fisher's Maritime Heritage Society Treasure Museum is opposite the Audubon House. Fascinating gold and silver jewelry and treasures from the Atocha are displayed. You can touch a gold bar. Gems and coins from the wreck have been fashioned into jewelry and may be purchased. Reproductions of the coins are sold too. Located at 200 Greene St., Key West FL 33040. Phone: 305-294-9936.

The Key West Lighthouse Museum is Florida's third oldest brick lighthouse. Climb 88 steps and view the entire city from the observation level. Great photo opportunities. Located at 938 Whitehead Street, Key West FL 33040. Phone 305-294-0012.

The Key West Aquarium, opened in 1932, was the first tourism attraction built in the Florida Keys. The exhibit includes a living reef, displays of sharks, barracudas, angel fish and a turtle pool. There is a touch tank. A huge plastic shark outside makes a patient souvenir-photo subject. The aquarium is on the waterfront at Mallory. The entrance is behind the shops. Phone: 305-296-2051. Write to One Whitehead Street, Key West FL 33040.

Turtle Kraals is operated as a waterside restaurant featuring a variety of turtles for viewing only. The huge loggerhead turtles are protected and no longer harvested as food. Other denizens of the deep such as shark, rays and octopus can be seen. There is also a touch tank for children. Located at Two Lands End Village, Key West FL 33040. Phone: 305-294- 0176.

Hemingway House was home to Ernest Hemingway and his second wife Pauline from 1931 to 1961. Now a registered national historic landmark, the house and gardens are where Hemingway wrote *For Whom the Bell Tolls, Green Hills of Africa, A Farewell to Arms, The Fifth Column* and *Snows of Kilimanjaro*. Descendents of Hemingway's cats roam the tropical grounds. Located at 907 Whitehead Street.

Fort Zachary Taylor State Park and Beach. Open 8 am to sunset. A stronghold during the Civil War, the fort displays the largest collection of Civil War cannons in the U.S. It's off Duval St. Visitors with cars pay $2.50 for the vehicle and driver, plus $1.50 per passenger. Picnic grills. Spectacular sunsets.

Fort Jefferson National Monument is 70 miles west of Key West and may be reached by boat or seaplane. Self-guided tours of the fort are combined with snorkeling, sightseeing, camping, and birdwatching. For boating information call the Coast Guard Base: 305-247-6211. For flights contact Key West Seaplane Service, 5603 Junior College Road, Stock Island FL 33040. Phone: 305-294-6978.

The Key West Cemetery, like the native inhabitants of this tiny, subtropical island, is unique. Filled with humor and history, one stone reads: "I Told You I Was Sick." Carved into another headstone at a nearby grave is the self-consoling, tongue-in-cheek, message of a grieving widow: "At Least I Know Where He's Sleeping Tonight." At a special memorial in the cemetery rest the bodies of those who died when the U.S. battleship *Maine* was sunk in Havana's Harbor in 1898, touching off the Spanish-American War. The cemetery fills 21 prime acres in the heart of the historic district.

Sunset Celebration. If one attraction is a must for a Key West visit, it is the sunset at Mallory Square Pier. The place comes alive

*Southernmost
Point*

with entertainment. There is a unicyclist wriggling free of a straight jacket, two men tumbling while a woman beats out a tune on a washboard and cymbals. A juggler delights the crowd first with oranges, then with flaming Indian clubs. Another juggler, after beating out rhythms on a bongo drum, dazzles the crowd with a tossed machete and flaming stick. If you're hungry, the Cookie Lady seems to sense it, arriving on her bicycle from which she hawks warm brownies and cookies.

The entertainment is free, but the entertainers do pass the hat. The standard pitch of two jugglers is: "We welcome your dollars. We welcome your complaints. If you have any complaints, write them on a five-dollar bill and put the bill in the plate." There are no complaints, but plenty of applause, loudest when the Key West sun drops into the sea.

At the Fish House Restaurant, Key Largo

Quay Beach Club, Key Largo

Duval St. at night, from La Concha rooftop

DINING

Seafood, always abundant in the waters of the Gulf of Mexico and Florida Keys, has dictated many local food habits and preferences. Yellowtail, red snapper, shrimp, dolphin (the fish) and stone crab claws are prominent menu features. All come from local waters.

The alligator has been brought back from near extinction, in part, to make a nightly appearance as a house specialty—fried or broiled. But, if your tastes don't run toward exotic, avoid dishes labeled "mixed seafood grill".

Stone crab claws are quite delectable and in some minds ecologically sound, as just one claw is removed from the live crab which is then thrown back into the sea. The claw grows back. Divers and snorkelers exploring the reefs spot these curious crabs brandishing one huge claw and one tiny one.

Bahama food such as fish stew served with grits or bollos (pronounced bow-yows), an adaptation of Southern hush puppies made with mashed, shelled black-eyed peas instead of ground corn meal, is featured in many restaurants.

A local dessert favorite is Key lime pie, made with condensed milk and the juice and minced rind of piquant Key limes which flourish in the area.

As the population of the area has grown and as tourism has grown to attract more than two million visitors a year, exotic dining inroads have been made. There now are restaurants featuring Polynesian, Chinese, German, French, Greek and Italian cuisine.

As in any seaside area, raw bars are prominent. You will find oysters and clams but conch is king. Served grilled, ground in burgers, fried in batters as fritters and raw in conch salad, it's all part of the local scene along with wonderful, chewy crisp squid rings done in batter and deep-fried in a continental, Mediterranean manner.

Cuban-influenced dishes are gaining in popularity. Favorites are flavored meats such as *lechon*, a roast of pork pungently flavored with garlic and tart sour oranges, *ropa vieja* (old clothes), a left-over dish, *vaca frita*, literally fried cow, and *picadillo*, a hamburger-caper-cum-raisin concoction in a savory sauce. All are usually served with boiled white or yellow rice, flavored with saffron, and black beans.

Try them all. You'll find the south Florida cuisine a delight.

EVERGLADES

In Everglades City don't miss dinner at the historic **Rod and Gun Club**. Once an exclusive hideaway for statesmen and movie stars, it is now a first-rate gourmet restaurant. Pass up seating in the cypress-panelled dining room for a table on the veranda overlooking the Barron River where you'll be serenaded by croaking frogs and alligators, singing birds and other whimsical sounds of the swamp. Watch wading birds and boaters stream into the sunset (813-695-2101). Seafood and steak dishes start at $15. Open for breakfast and dinner. No credit cards.

The Last Frontier Restaurant is at the edge of town on Rte. 29. House dinner specials are fried fish, steaks, Frontier burgers, shrimp and frog legs. Excellent southern breakfasts are served from 6 am on. Open Sun. till Wed. 6 am till 4 pm, Thurs., Fri. and Sat. till 9 pm. No credit cards.

For a a fast lunch or dinner mixed with a bit of nostalgia, try **Susies Ice Cream Parlor**. A right turn at the schoolyard off the Rte. 29 circle will bring you to this historic site. Built in 1921 by Barron Collier as the community laundry building, the structure retains the typical appearance of Everglades City in the 1920's. Back then the town known as "Everglades" was the seat of the county government and served as a company outpost run by Barron Collier, a wealthy ad man. The once-bustling fishing port lost its status when World War II and the depression hit. No credit cards.

Oyster House Restaurant on Rte. 29 is a family restaurant which features local seafood and carry-out service for breakfast, lunch or dinner (813-695-2073). Most dinners $10 to $15. No credit cards.

The Miccosukee Indian Village Restaurant, adjacent to Shark Valley on the Tamiami Trail, offers a variety of Indian dishes from a Miccosukee burger to a typical American menu (305-223-8388 or 223-8380).

Flamingo

Flamingo Lodge (305-253-2241) offers seafood and steaks at low to moderate prices. It is the only restaurant in Everglades National Park located at the end of the Main Park Road.

THE FLORIDA KEYS

Key Largo

Key Largo is fast-food heaven with popular chain restaurants everywhere. For all-day diving or fishing excursions there are grocery stores and even gas stations that offer packaged lunches and cold beverages to go.

Mr. Submarine, MM 100, oceanside, has subs, gyros and yogurts. **Tower of Pizza**, MM 100, oceanside, delivers New York style pizza—(305-451-1461). Sit down service.

For a unique tropical atmosphere and superb gourmet cuisine try the **Quay Restaurant**, MM 102.5, bayside (305-451-0943). Indoor or garden seating. Moderate to expensive. Adjacent is the **Quay Mesquite Grill** which serves excellent fried or broiled fish sandwiches. The complex also features a freshwater pool, boat docks, beachside bar and entertainment. Sunset cruises.

Everglades Rod and Gun Club Restaurant

Romantic, starlight seating and gourmet seafood are also found at **Snooks Bayside Club**, MM 99.9 (305-451-3070). Moderate to expensive. Garden patio or indoor dining. The **Fish House**, oceanside at MM 102.4, serves fresh fish, steaks and chicken for lunch or dinner. Moderate prices. Excellent. Casual.

Try the **Cracked Conch**, MM 105, oceanside (305-451-0732) for conch fitters and fried alligator, 90 different beers and honey biscuits. Low to moderate.

Rick & Debbie's Tugboat, oceanside at MM 100, is a locals' favorite. Specials are fried or broiled fish. Low to moderate.

Harbour House, at MM 90.3 (305-852-7222), offers seafood salads and lunch specialties.

Early breakfasts are served at **Howard Johnsons**, MM 102.5 (305-451-2032), **Harriets**, MM 95.7 (305-852-8689), **Holiday Inn**, MM 100, and **Gilberts**, MM 107.9 (305-451-1133).

Islamorada

Islamorada's grills sizzle with fresh seafood and the most unique dining experiences in the Keys. You'll find the hot spot for fast food on the shores of Holiday Isle, MM 84 oceanside. Food stands line this beach complex with barbecued everything. Ice cream and pretzel vendors crowd in alongside the Keys' most dazzling display of string bikinis. Or take the elevator to the sixth-floor restaurant for a more quiet view of the sea. Prices rise with the elevation—starting at $13.

In the same complex, roadside, is **Rip's Hot Rock Cafe**. Diners at Rip's prepare their own entrees on thick granite slabs which are heated to 600° and brought to your table. Your waitress supplies you with hot garlic bread, fresh, ready-to-cook vegetables and a choice of sirloin, chicken or shrimp, or a combination. Just toss a little salt on your rock and give your food a turn or two until it looks right. A choice of sauces adds the finishing touch. It's easy. Can't handle it? Try the ribs. They're served cooked.

Enjoy sunset over the bay and fresh seafood at **Lorelei Restaurant**, MM 82, bayside. The outdoor **Cabana Bar** features burgers, fish sandwiches and a raw bar. Entertainment on weekends. Drive or boat to it.

Marker 88 offers exotic fish and steak entrees in a romantic setting. Choose from Scampi Mozambique, Snapper Rangoon, Lobster Marco Polo and a host of other gourmet creations. Closed Mondays. Reservations a must (305-852-9315). MM 88, Plantation Key. Expensive.

Whale Harbor Restaurant features an all-you-can-eat seafood buffet nightly. Huge selection. Lovely setting in the old Islamorada lighthouse, adjacent to the Islamorada docks at MM 83.5. Moderate.

Try a hand-tossed pizza or pasta at **Woody's**, MM 82 (305-664-4335). Family dining in the early evening. Late night food with adult entertainment every night but Monday. Inexpensive.

Cheeca Lodge offers casual dining at the **Ocean Terrace Grill**, MM 81.5 (305-664-4651). Moderate to expensive.

The Green Turtle Inn, MM 81.5, has an old time Keys atmosphere and excellent cuisine. Wood-paneled walls are covered with celebrity photos. Leave room for their rum pie. Gets crowded after 6 pm; (305-664-9595). Closed Mondays.

For a quick meal try a pita sandwich at the **Ice Cream Stoppe**, MM 80.5 (305-664-5026).

Long Key

Little Italy Restaurant at MM 68.5 serves early breakfasts, lunch and dinner. Italian specialties, fresh seafood and steaks in a cozy atmosphere. Low to moderate; (305-664-4472).

Marathon

Marathon is a heavily-populated community with a wide choice of restaurants. The best in atmosphere and fine dining is **Kelsey's** at MM 48.5 (305-743-9018). Moderate to expensive.

The Hurricane Raw Bar & Restaurant at MM 49.5 features over 6,000 sq. ft. of raw bar, two cocktail bars, two dining rooms, and live entertainment. Specialties are hot and spicy chicken wings, fresh clams, oysters and conch (305-743-5755). Moderate.

Fishing guides and boat captains swap tales at the **Anglers**, MM 48, above Kelsey's at Faro Blanco Resort. Open for lunch and dinner (305-743-9018). Moderate.

Enjoy indoor or outdoor patio dining, bayside, at the **Quay of Marathon**, MM 54 (305-289-1810). Poolside lunch or dinners are available at **Hawks Cay Cantina** at MM 61 on Duck Key. Full handicapped facilities. Moderate.

Fast, take-out food at low prices is featured at **Porky's Too** on the Marathon side of the Seven Mile Bridge.

Sugarloaf Key

Enjoy grilled seafood on the porch of a 1935 stone house at **Mangrove Mama's**, MM 20. Open for lunch and dinner (305-745-3030). Moderate.

Key West

The locals' favorite watering hole in Key West is **The Half Shell Raw Bar** at Land's End Village. Menu features are fried or broiled fish, shrimp and conch, raw oysters and clams. Friendly service. Try for a table on the back porch, overlooking the water, where you'll spot six or seven huge tarpon (305-294-7496). Open for lunch and dinner. Moderate.

Across the wharf is **Turtle Kraals Bar and Restaurant**, offering fresh fish, lobster and the largest selection of imported beers in Key West (305-294-2640). The restaurant is what remains of the days when turtle were brought in by the boat load from as far away as the Cayman Islands and Nicaragua.

Kraals is an Afrikan word meaning holding pen or enclosure. It refers to the concrete pilings that were driven into the ocean bottom to form a holding pen for the turtles until they could be shipped to the Northeast or slaughtered and made into soup in the cannery. Today the cannery buildings have been restored into Key West's most unique restaurant. Lunch and dinner.

The best breakfasts in the Keys are served at **Pepe's Cafe**, 806 Caroline St. Frosted glasses of fresh orange juice, and artfully-prepared French toast or egg dishes are served indoors or outside under a canopy of flowering vines. Outdoor decor includes a white picket fence with peep holes at two levels—one for people and one for pets (305-294-7192).

The **Rooftop Lounge** at Holiday Inn's La Concha on Duval Street serves exotic island drinks and is the best spot in town for sunset viewing.

Two **Mr. Submarines** serve hot and cold subs—1800 N. Roosevelt Blvd and 12 Duval St.

Mallory Market is the center of the Historic Key West Waterfront and offers every imaginable, fast-food service. After touring the square, munch on hot dogs and ice cream at the **Old Fisherman's Cafe.**

Duval Street is lined with wonderful cafes and restaurants featuring varied, ethnic dishes. **El Cacique**, 125 Duval St., specializes in Cuban cuisine: roast pork, palomila steak, and paella (305-294-4000). Open for breakfast, lunch and dinner. Low to moderate. Or try **Gringo's Cantina** on 509 1/2 Duval St. for spicy Mexican cuisine (305-294-9215).

Exotic dishes from Southeast Asia are found at **Dim Sum**, 613 Duval St. in the rear (305-294-6230).

Louis's Back Yard, located at the corner of Vernon & Waddell Streets, is one of Key West's finest waterfront restaurants. American cuisine highlights the menu for lunch, dinner and Sunday brunch (305-294-1061). Expensive. **Cafe at Louie's** (second floor) serves Nuevo Cubano cooking.

Foley Square has two restaurants, two patio and garden areas offering seafood, Cajun food, deli sandwiches, char-burgers, pizza and a raw bar. Disco and live entertainment at 218 Duval St (305-294-4383).

Affordable prices and Italian favorites are found at **Aunt Rose's,** 1900 Flagler St. (305-294-6214).

Named for Ernest Hemingway's favorite 1930's bar (actually across the street) **Sloppy Joe's** is a Key West tradition. The huge building vibrates with live music and memorabilia. At the corner of Duval and Greene Sts.

ACCOMMODATIONS

Resort and motel rates vary with the time of year, the high season being mid-December to mid-April. Check with your travel agent for money-saving packages. Several tour operators offer four-day or longer stays that include airfare, meals and diving or fishing. Rates drop considerably for stays longer than seven days.

Day Rates: Low, $45 to $65 per person. Moderate, $75 to $105; Deluxe: $110 and up.

Major credit cards are accepted at all of the resorts and large motels. Some of the smaller motels ask for cash only. All hotels listed have air conditioning and color TV.

EVERGLADES NATIONAL PARK

Please note that although the park is open year round, the recreational services are open from mid November to Mid April.

Flamingo Lodge, Marina & Outpost Resort is the only lodging inside Everglades National Park. Get there by taking Florida Turnpike or Route 1 to Florida City then follow signs to Everglades National Park and Flamingo. It takes about 45 minutes to drive the 38-mile distance from the main entrance to Flamingo. Rooms are air-conditioned, modern and comfortable. Freshwater pool. Absolutely no pets. Full service from November 1 through April 30. Moderate. Phone: 305-253-2241. Write to P.O. Box 428, Flamingo FL 33030.

Additional motel and resorts near to the main park area exist in Homestead and Florida City. For up-dated listings contact the Greater Homestead-Florida City Chamber of Commerce, 650 US Hwy 1, Homestead FL 33030. Phone: 305-247-2332.

For the north western, Ten Thousand Islands region contact Everglades Area Chamber of Commerce, P.O. Box 130, Everglades City, FL 33929, (813) 695-3941.

Camping

Camping in Everglades National Park is on a first-come, first-served basis. Long Pine Key has 108 sites, Flamingo has 235 drive-in sites and 60 walk-in sites for tents. Fees are $8.00 per night for the regular sites, $4.00 per night for the Flamingo walk-in sites. Group campsites are $10.00 per night at both locations (maximum 15 people) and may be reserved in advance. Camping is restricted to 14 days per visit and a total of 30 days per year. Arrive early to obtain a site. Checkout time is 10 am. There are no water or electrical hookups. Restrooms, drinking water and sanitary dump stations are at both campgrounds; cold water showers at Flamingo only. Limited groceries and camping supplies may be purchased at the Flamingo Marina Store. Long Pine Key has no camp store and all supplies must be obtained in Homestead. Pets are allowed at the campgrounds.

Backcountry Camping

Backcountry Use Permits are required for all overnight use of the backcountry (except on board boats) and may be obtained at Flamingo and Everglades City ranger stations. Most sites are chickees—elevated wooden platforms with a roof and chemical toilet—and accessible only by boat. Length of stay and number of people are restricted. Pets are not allowed on developed trails or in the backcounry.

NORTHERN EVERGLADES
Ten Thousand Island Region

This jungle-like area of mangrove islands borders Everglades National Park and is most frequented by fishermen and canoe campers seeking an untouched-wilderness experience. Sightseeing and airboat excursions featuring alligator-, manatee-, and frog-watching outings are popular attractions. For additional accommodations and activities in this area contact Everglades Area Chamber of Commerce, P.O. Box E, Everglades City FL 33929. Phone: 813-695-3941.

Everglades' Rod and Gun Resort Lodge Motel accommodations, heated pool, waterfront restaurant, lounge and full-service marina. No pets. Write to P.O. Box 190, Everglades City FL 33929. Phone: 813-695-2101.

Port of the Islands Resort offers deluxe, sportsman accommodations, an RV park, a trap and skeet range, pool, tennis and sightseeing cruises. No pets. Phone: US 1-800-237-4173, FL 1-800-282-3011, 813-394-3101.

Sportsman's Club has motel rooms and efficiencies. Some small, quiet pets allowed. Call first. Write P.O. Box 399 (318 Mamie St), Chokoloskee FL 33925. Phone: 813-695-4224.

Camping

Outdoor Resorts is an RV campground well-suited for boaters. Forty eight of the 283 sites have dockage on the bay. Additional dockage for 65 boats. All sites are landscaped with paved drives and patios. Fully-equipped marina with boat ramp, bait shop, boat rental, three pools, spa with saunas, tennis. Motel. Pets are allowed in the campground, but not in the motel. Write P.O. Box 429, Chokoloskee FL 33925. Phone: FL 1-800-282-9028, 813-695-2881.

Glades Haven at the Everglades City entrance to Everglades National Park offers tent and RV sites are offered. The campground features ocean access, dockage, boat ramp, bath and showers and club house. Home of North American Canoe Tours. Write 800 S.E. Copeland Ave., Everglades City FL 33929. Phone: 813-695-2746.

FLORIDA KEYS

You will find whatever type accommodations you prefer in the Keys. There are casual, informal housekeeping cottages, simply-furnished bayside motels, spacious, condo and house rentals, luxurious resort

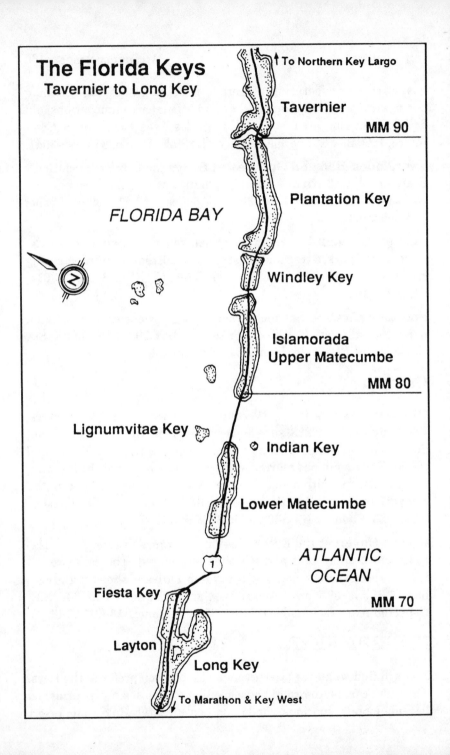

villages, houseboats, and campgrounds, most of which are packed with RV's. All accommodations are air-conditioned and most have cable-color TV and a refrigerator in the room.

Some of the older mom-and-pop motels on the bay have been updated and restored and offer a certain island charm that is hard to duplicate in the large resorts. A few are badly in need of renovation and also are parking areas for RV's. Send for current brochures.

Key Largo Accommodations

For a complete list of home rental agencies Contact the Key Largo Chamber of Commerce, 105950 Overseas Hwy., Key Largo FL 33037. Phone: 305-451-1414, US 800-822-1088.

Anchorage Resort & Yacht Club is bayside at the northern most tip of Key Largo, away fromthe mainstream of activity. The resort features a fishing pier, laundry, tennis court and deck. Balconies, grills, and a deck. Boat docking. Deluxe. Write 107800 Overseas Hwy, Key Largo FL 33037. Phone: 305-451-0500

Best Western Suites, located oceanside on a canal, is a two-story resort. Apartments have with modern kitchen facilitiesand screened in patios. Boat docking. Group discounts and dive packages available. No pets. Write MM 100, 201 Ocean Drive, Key Largo FL 33037. Phone: 800-528-1234 or 305-451-5081.

Holiday Inn Key Largo Resort is adjacent to a large marina with a boat ramp and docking for all size craft. The resort has been updated and features comfortable rooms, restaurant, gift shop, freshwater pool with waterfalls and fast access to diving and recreation facilities. It is also the home of the *African Queen* used in the 1951 movie starring Humphrey Bogart and Katharine Hepburn. No pets. Moderate to deluxe. Write MM 100, 99701 Overseas Hwy, Key Largo FL 33037. Phone: US 800-THE-KEYS or 305-451-2121.

Howard Johnson's Resort in Key largo is bayside. Features are modern, nicely decorated rooms, swimming in the pool or bay, sand beach, restaurant, pool, balconies, beach bar, dock, dive and other packages. Color cable TV. Refrigerators and microwaves. Some small pets are allowed. Call first. Group rates available. Write MM 102, P.O. Box 1024, Key Largo FL 33037. Phone: 800-654-2000 or 305-451-1400.

Island Bay Resort, bayside at MM 92.5, is a small motel with kitchen facilities, a boat dock and ramp, sandy beach and cable TV. No pets. Write P.O. Box 573, Tavernier FL. Phone: 305-852-4087. Moderate.

Kelly's Motel at MM 104.5 is located on a sheltered cove. Boat dock and ramp. Dive trips. Sandy beach. Cooking facilities. No pets. Write 104220 Overseas Hwy., Key Largo FL 33037. Phone: 305-451-1622. Low.

Keys Motel is on the old Overseas Highway at MM 90.5 in Tavernier. Eighteen units. You can dock your boat at the adjacent deep water canal. No ramp. No pets. Kitchen facilities available. Low to Moderate. Write 90611 Old Highway, Tavernier FL 33070. Phone: 305-852-2351.

Kona Kai Resort at MM 97.8 is a nine-unit motel on the bay. Color cable TV, phones, fishing pier. Boat dock and ramp. No pets. Write 97802 Overseas Highway, Key Largo FL 33037. Phone: 305-852-7200. Low to Moderate.

Largo Lodge at MM 101.5 is a charming, bayside complex offering six apartments—all in a tropical garden setting. Guests must be at least 16 years old. Swimming. Small boat dock. Ramp. No pets. Write 101740 Overseas Highway, Key Largo FL 33037. Phone: 800-IN-THE-SUN (468-4378) or 305-451-0424. Moderate.

Marina Del Mar is a luxury dive resort on a deepwater marina in the heart of Key Largo. There are 130 rooms, suites and villas. Refrigerators in all rooms. The suites have complete kitchens. Rooms overlook the yacht basin or ocean. Dive shop on premises. Fishing charters. Meeting facilities. Waterfront restaurant and lounge. Write P.O. Box 1050, Key Largo FL 33037. Phone: 305-451-4107, US 800-451-3483, FL 800-253-3483, Canada 800-638-3483. Moderate to deluxe.

Popps Motel on the bay at MM 95.5 has 10 units with cooking facilities, a small beach, boat dock and ramp. No pets. Write P.O. Box 43, Key Largo FL 33037. Phone: 305-852-5201. Moderate.

Port Largo Villas in the heart of Key Largo are two-bedroom, two-bath units with cable TV, jacuzzis, tennis court, sundeck. No pets. Write P.O. Box 1290, Key Largo FL 33037. Phone: 305-451-4847. Deluxe.

Rock Reef Resort at MM 98 offers clean, comfortable cottages and apartments on the bay with one, two, or three bedrooms. Playground, tropical gardens. Boat dock and ramp. Sandy beach. No pets. Write P.O. Box 73, Key Largo FL. Phone: 800-477-2343 or 305-852-2401. Low.

Sheraton Key Largo is a watersports resort with 200 luxury rooms, restaurants, lounge, nature trails, two pools and a large dock on the bay. Private beach. Meeting facilities. No pets. Write 97000 US Hwy 1, Key Largo FL 33037. Phone: 305-852-5553; worldwide 800-800-325-3535; FL 800-826-1006. Deluxe.

Stone Ledge Resort, bayside, is a quiet, 19-unit motel with comfortable rooms, sandy beach, boat dock. Ten of the units have kitchens. Refrigerators in all rooms. TV. No pets. Write P.O. Box 50, Key Largo FL 33037. Phone: 305-852-8114.

Tropic Vista Motel at MM 90.5 is on a canal, oceanside. Dive shop on premises. Dock. Pets allowed in some rooms. Call first. Write P.O. Box 88, Tavernier FL 33070. Phone: 800-537-3253 or 305-852-8799.

Key Largo Rv & Tent Campgrounds

America Outdoors. MM 97.5. Sandy beach, laundry, bath houses. Boat dock, ramp and marina. RV sites. Pets allowed. Write 97450 Overseas Hwy., Key Largo FL 33037. Phone: 305-852-8054.

Blue Lagoon Resort & Marina, MM 99.5, bayside, rents and parks RVs. A couple of simple efficiencies for rent also. Parking is tight, but you are in the heart of Key Largo. Boat dock. Swimming. Pets ok. Write 99096 US Hwy 1, Key Largo FL 33037. Phone: 305-451-2908.

Calusa Camp Resort. MM 101.5. Bayside waterfront RV park. Boat dock, ramp, marina, bait shop, camp store. Rentals. Pets allowed. Write 325 Calusa, Key Largo FL 33037. Phone: 800-457-2267 or 305-451-0232.

Campers Cove. MM 101.6. Bayside. Write 101640 US Hwy 1, Key Largo FL. Phone: 305-451-0561.

Key Largo Kampground. MM 101.5. Oceanfront RV and tent sites, boat dock, ramp, laundry and bath house. Write P.O. Box 118-A, Key Largo FL 33037. Phone: 305-451-1431, US 800-KAMP-OUT.

Point Laura Campground & Marina. MM 112.5. Located six miles north of Key Largo's main area, this campground is best described as a sprawling marina with RV parking. It is somewhat isolated, but has fuel and a bath house. Dockage. Ramp. Mosquitos. Pets allowed. Write 999 Morris Lane, Cross Key FL 33037. Phone: 305-451-0033.

Islamorada Accommodations

Plantation Key to Long Key

For a complete list of home rental agencies Contact the Islamorada Chamber of Commerce, P.O. Box 915, Islamorada FL 33036. Phone: 305-664-4503

Breezy Palms Resort, MM 80, on the ocean, offers one-, two-and three-room villas, beach cottages or studio efficiencies. All with well-equipped kitchens attractive furnishings. Maid service. Large swimming beach. Fresh water pool, boat harbor and ramp with a light dock for night fishing. No pets. Write P.O. Box 767, Islamorada FL 33036. Phone: 305-664-2361/664-2371.

Caloosa Cove Resort, MM 73.8, offers 30 deluxe, oceanfront condos, one or two bedroom with modern kitchens. Pool, lounge, restaurant, tennis, boat rentals, free breakfast and activities. Full service marina with dockage. No pets. Write 73801 US Hwy 1, Islamorada FL 33036. Phone: 305-664-8811.

Cheeca Lodge offers pampered seclusion, oceanside, at MM 82. Well described at being in "its own neighborhood", the resort offers guests a wealth of activities including dive and snorkeling trips, a nine-hole golf course, sailing, fishing, tennis, parasailing, windsurfing complete with a staff of expert instructors, captains or pros. Features include oversized guestrooms and villas, most with private balconies and paddle fans, a children's recreational camp, shops, gourmet dining, entertainment, palm-lined swimming/snorkeling beach, pool, 525-foot lighted fishing pier. Dockage and marina. Conference center. No pets. Deluxe. Write P.O. Box 527, Islamorada FL 33036. Phone: 305-664-4651 or 800-327-2888.

Chesapeake of Whale Harbor, adjacent to the Whale Harbor Restaurant and Islamorada docks, is on six oceanfront acres at MM 83.5. The modern resort offers motel or efficiency units, a sand beach and deep water lagoon. Walk to fishing charter boat docks. No pets. Write P.O. Box 909, Islamorada Fl 33036. Phone: 800-338-3395 or 305-664-4662. Moderate to Deluxe.

El Capitan Resort, MM 84, offers efficiencies for two to six people in the Holiday Isle complex. Oceanside lagoon and beach. Boat dockage. No pets. Write MM 84, Islamorada FL 33036. Phone: 305-664-2321, US 800-327-7070. Moderate to deluxe.

Holiday Isle Resort encompasses an entire beach club community with every imaginable watersport and activity. Guests choose from rooms, efficiencies or suites. The beach vibrates with reggae music. Vendors offer parasailing, fishing and diving charters, sailing, wind-surfing, jetskiing, inflatable-island rentals, sun lounges and dancing. Fast food stands offering barbecued dishes, pizza, ice cream, drinks and more are scattered about the grounds. There is a lovely rooftop restaurant and an unique cook-it-yourself-on-slabs-of-granite place in the parking lot. Rooms are luxurious. The beach is open to everyone and is packed early during the high season. No pets. Write 84001 US Hwy 1, Islamorada FL. Phone: 305-664-2321, US 800-327-7070.

Harbor Lights Motel, oceanfront, is part of the Holiday Isle beach complex offering efficiencies, rooms and cottages. Write 84001 US Hwy 1, Islamorada FL. Phone: 800-327-7070.

Howard Johnsons Resort is oceanside at MM 84.5 adjacent to Holiday Isle. Nice sand beach, restaurant. Guests wander back and forth to Holiday Isle beach. Boat dock and ramp. No pets. Write 84001 US Hwy 1, Islamorada FL 33036. Phone: US 800-654-2000. Moderate to Deluxe.

La Jolla Resort is bayside and offers a quiet, tropical garden atmosphere. Kitchen units are comfortable. Boat dock and ramp. Small swimming beach, grills. Some pets with restrictions. Call first. Write Box 51, Islamorada Fl 33036. Phone: 305-664-9213. Low to Moderate.

Lime Tree Bay Resort at MM 68.5 is an older motel, but comfortable with beautiful grounds. Kitchen units available. There is a restaurant, tennis court, boat dock and beach with a fresh water pool. No pets. Write P.O. Box 839, Long Key FL 33001. Phone: 305-664-4740. Low to Moderate.

Ocean 80 Inc., MM 80, oceanside, features luxury efficiencies or suites with fully-equipped kitchens. Tiki bar, restaurant, tennis, pool and jet-ski rentals. Adjacent to full service marina. Boat dock. No pets. P.O. Box 949 Islamorada FL 33036. Phone: 305-664-4411. US 800-367-9050.

Plantation Yacht Harbor Resort, MM 87, bayside, is a sprawling resort complex with tennis courts, private beach, jet skis and a huge marina with protected docking for large and small craft. A dive shop and lovely restaurant overlook the bay. No pets. Write 87000 US Hwy 1, Plantation Key, Islamorada FL 33036. Phone: 305-852-2381. Moderate to deluxe.

Tropical Reef Resort, MM 85, oceanside, offers three fresh-water pools (one childsized), picnic beach with tiki huts and floating breakfast cafe, marina and boat rentals. No pets. Write 849 US 1, Islamorada FL 33036. Phone: 305-664-8881 or 800-654-9748, FL 800-843-9810. Low to deluxe.

Marathon Accommodations

For a complete list of rental units, condos and villas contact the Greater Marathon Chamber of Commerce, 3330 US Hwy 1, Marathon FL 33050. Phone: 305-743-5417 or 800-842-9580

Banana Bay Resort & Marina, MM 49.5, bayside, features 60 rooms, tennis, charter fishing and diving, pool and conference room. Boat ramp and dock. No pets. Write 4590 US Hwy 1, Marathon FL 33050. Phone: 800-448-6636 or 305-743-3500. Moderate.

Buccaneer Resort, MM 48.5, bayside, has 76 units, beach, cafe, tennis, boat dock and charters. Some kitchen units. Write 2600 US Hwy 1, Marathon Fl 33050. Phone: 305-743-9071, US 800-237-3329, FL 800-843-1799. Low to moderate.

Conch Key Cottages, MM 62.3, oceanside, are situated on a secluded, private island which up until recently could only be reached by boat. New owners have built a landfill roadway so you can drive the short distance from US 1. Rustic, wooden cottages have screened-in porches and huge ceiling fans. Pool. All air-conditioned, the cottages feature well-equipped, knotty pine kitchens, cable TV, hammock and barbecue. Coin washer and dryers on premises. Boat dock and ramp. Well behaved pets are welcome. Call first. Write Box 424, Marathon FL 33050. Phone: 800-330-1877 or 305-289-1377. Moderate to deluxe.

Holiday Inn of Marathon, MM 54, oceanside, has 134 rooms, restaurant, and bar. Boat ramp and marina. Pets ok. Write 13201 US Hwy 1, Marathon FL 33050. Phone: 800-224-5053 or 800-HOLIDAY. Moderate.

Faro Blanco Marine Resort, MM 48, spreads over two shores with the most diverse selection of facilities on the Atlantic and the Gulf. Choose from houseboat suites, condos, garden cottages, or an apartment in the Faro Blanco lighthouse for a special treat. There is a full-service marina if you are arriving by yacht and wish to tie up for a stay. Dockmaster stands by on VHF Channel 16. Convenient to fine restaurants and diving. Pets allowed in the houseboats and cottages, but not the condos. Children under 18 not allowed in the condos. Write 1996 US Hwy 1, Marathon FL 33050. Phone: 800-759-3276. Moderate to Deluxe.

Hawks Cay Resort and Marina offers 177 spacious rooms and suites. Heated pool, saltwater lagoon with sandy beach, 18-hole golf course nearby, marine-mammal training center featuring dolphin shows for guests. Charter fishing and diving boats leave from the marina. Protected boat slips for large and small craft. No pets. Write MM 61, Duck Key, FL 33050. Phone: 305-743-7000, FL 800-432-2242. Ultra deluxe.

Howard Johnsons Resort, MM 54, bayside has a private beach, dive shop, dock and marina, restaurant. Pets ok. Write 13351 US Hwy 1, Marathon FL 33050. Phone: 800-654-2000 or 305-743-8550. Moderate.

Kingsail Resort Motel, MM 50. Bayside accommodations range from modern, attractive rooms to well-equipped efficiencies and one-bedroom apartments. There is a boat ramp, dock, grocer, pool, shaded Tiki. No pets. Fishing and diving charters. Write P.O. box 986, Marathon FL 33050. Phone: 305-743-5246, FL 800-423-7474. Low to moderate.

Rainbow Bend Fishing Resort, oceanside at MM 58, offers free use of a motorboat or sailboat with every room plus complimentary breakfast daily. There is a wide sandy beach, pool, fishing pier, tackle shop. Dive and fishing charters. Rooms and efficiencies. Cafe. Pets ok. Write P.O. Box 2447, Grassy Key, FL 33050. Phone: 305-289-1505.

The **Seahorse Motel**, at MM 51, bayside, offers protected dock space, a playground, pool, barbecue patio, quiet rooms and efficiencies. Write 7196 US Hwy 1, Marathon FL 33050. Phone: 305-743-6571.

Big Pine Key

Big Pine is centered between Marathon and Key West. A twenty minute drive will get you to either.

Big Pine Resort Motel, located at MM 30.5 bayside, offers the serenity of an out island with nearby proximity to Looe Key Marine Sanctuary. The motel has 32 large and comfortable motel rooms, efficiencies and apartments. Adjacent restaurant. No pets Rt 5, Box 796, Big Pine Key FL 33043. Phone: 305-872-9090.

Little Torch Key

Little Palm Island. Located on an out island, this deluxe resort offers all recreational facilities: day sailer, windsurfers, fishing gear, snorkel gear, canoes and bicycles. Suites include private balcony, ceiling fans, air conditioning, coffee maker, refrigerator, wet bar and whirlpool. Launch transfers to the island are provided. No TV or phones. Write to Overseas Highway 1, MM 28.5, Route 4, Box 1036, Little Torch Key, FL 33042. Phone: 1-800 GET LOST (343-8567) or 305-872-2524.

Sugarloaf Key

Sugarloaf Lodge, at MM 17 bayside is a complete resort with miniature golf, airstrip, restaurant, boat rentals, fishing charters, tennis, pool and marina. Moderate. P.O. Box 148 Sugarloaf Key FL 33044. Phone: 305-745-3211.

Key West

To be near attractions stay in Old Town, for beaches choose S. Roosevelt Blvd accommodations. Lower rates are found on N. Roosevelt Blvd, the commercial area.

For a complete list of Key West accommodations including guest houses, condominiums and apartments and vacation homes contact the Greater Key West Chamber of Commerce, Mallory Square, 402 Wall St., Key West FL 33040. Phone: 800-LAST KEY or 305-294-2587.

Holiday Inn La Concha Hotel, 430 Duval St., Key West FL 33040. This historic hotel has been renovated in 1986 and is in the center of Old Town. Special features include 160 romantic rooms, a restaurant, fitness room, whirlpool spa, shops and the best view of the city from the rooftop lounge. Phone: 800-HOLIDAY or 305-296-2991. Handicapped accessible. Deluxe.

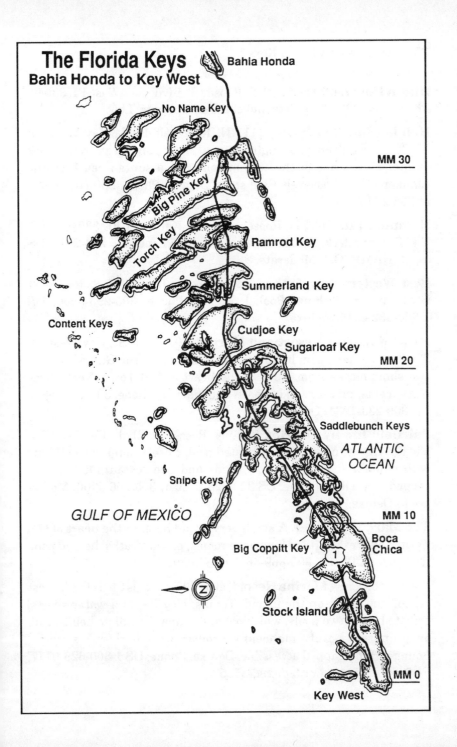

Hilton Haven Motel, 2319 N. Roosevelt Blvd, Key West FL 33040. Phone: 305-296-6925. Pets and children welcome. Low.

Holiday Inn Beachside, 1111 N. Roosevelt Blvd., Key West FL 33030. Located on your right as you enter Key West from Stock Island. This is one of the only motels with a suntan beach on the commercial N. Roosevelt Blvd strip. Deluxe. Phone: 800-HOLIDAY or 305-294-2571.

Hampton Inn, 2801 N. Roosevelt Blvd., Key West FL 33040. Pool, Tiki Bar, Sundeck. Handicapped accessible.Phone: 305-294-2917, US 1-800-HAMPTON. Moderate.

Best Western Key Ambassador Resort Inn, 3755 S. Roosevelt Blvd. Airport Pick-up. Pool, balconies. Phone: 305-296-3500, US 1-800-432-4315. Deluxe.

Hyatt Key West Resort and Marina, 601 Front St, Key West FL 33040. This 120-room luxury resort is located on the Gulf of Mexico, two short blocks from Dual in the heart of Old Town. Pool, three restaurants, private sandy beach and marina. Phone: 305-296-9900, US 800-233-1234. Deluxe.

Fairfield Inn by Marriot, 2400 N. Roosevelt Blvd., Key West FL 33040. One hundred rooms, heated pool, closest hotel to the Wharf with dolphin shows, sea lions, birds and two restaurants. Handicapped accessible. Phone: US 800-228-2800 or 305-296-5700. Moderate to Deluxe.

The Marquesa Hotel. A small very grand hotel in the heart of Old Town Key West. Fifteen luxurious rooms, private baths, heated pool. Restaurant. Phone: 800-869-4631 or 305-292-1919.

Marriott's Casa Marina Resort, at 1500 Reynolds St, is the largest oceanfront resort on the island. Tennis, bicycles, and water sports, private beach, two pools, whirlpool and sauna. Complete health club on premises. Lovely mahogany poolbar with barbecue services. Lounge. Handicapped accessible. Deluxe. Phone: US 1-800-626-0777, FL 1-800-235-4837 or 305-296-3535.

Ocean Key House on Mallory Square at Zero Duval St, offers deluxe suites on the Gulf of Mexico. Fully-equipped kitchens, jacuzzi. Private balcony with water and sunset views. VCR & movie rentals. No pets. Phone: US 800-328-9815, FL 800-231-9864.

Old Town Resorts, Inc. at 1319 Duval St in Old Town includes the Southernmost Motel in the US, the South Beach Oceanfront Motel, and the La Mer Hotel. Offers three pools, jacuzzi, Tiki Bar, sunning pier on the Atlantic, gift shop, dive shop, concierge. Walking distance to beach, shops, nightlife and dining. No pets. Moderate to deluxe. Phone: 305-296-6577, FL 1-800-354-4455.

Pegasus International Motel, 501 Southard St., Key West FL 33040. Old world service in Old Town at reasonable rates. 22 units. No pets. TV, private bath, air conditioning. Moderate. Phone: 800-397-8148 or 305-294-9323.

Pelican Landing, 915 Eisenhower Dr., Key West FL 33040. Marina suites sleep two to eight people. No pets. Full kitchens, pool, barbecue grills, Cable TV. Phone: 305-296-7583. Deluxe.

Pier House Hotel, One Duval St., Key West FL 33040. In the heart of Old Town Key West. Private beach, heated pool. Five restaurants, five bars, beachside entertainment. No pets. Phone: 305-296-4600, US 800-327-8340, FL 1-800-432-3414.

Ramada Inn, 3420 N. Roosevelt Blvd., Key West FL 33040. On the commercial strip across from the Gulf of Mexico. Air conditioned, Color TV, pool, tennis. Pets welcome. Handicapped accessible. Phone: 800-228-2828 or 305-294-5541 Moderate to Deluxe.

Marriot Reach Resort, 1435 Simonton St, Key West FL 33040. Phone 305-296-5000; US 1-800-874-4118. Elegant resort located on the only natural sand beach in Key West. 149 rooms (80 suites) each with a veranda, most with ocean view, ceiling fans, wet bar, Two restaurants, food store, library, five bars, entertainment. Health center, lap pool. Handicapped accessible. No pets. Deluxe.

Santa Maria Motel, 1401 Simonton St., Key West FL 33040. Phone: 800-821-KEYS or 305-296-5678. Charming motel close to Old Town. Olympic freshwater pool. Moderate.

Curry Mansion Inn, 511 Caroline St., Key West FL 33040. Nestled alongside the original 1899 Curry Mansion, the Inn offers 15 elegant romantic rooms, each opening onto a sparkling pool and surrounded by the lush foilage of the Curry Estate. Private baths and phones, wet bars, air conditioning, ceiling fans and TV. Deluxe. Phone: 305-294-5349.

Key West Campgrounds

Boyd's Campground, Maloney Ave., Stock Island FL 305- 294-1465. Southernmost Campground in the US on the Atlantic Ocean at Key West city limits. Features all watersports, showers restrooms, laundry, store, ice, city bus, telephone, dump station, bottle gas, electric, water, sewer hookups. Twenty boat slips and launching ramps Pool MC/Visa.

Jabour's Trailer Court, 223 Elizabeth, St., Key West FL 33040. Waterfront campground in Old Town Key West. Walking distance to everything. Tent and RVs welcome. Efficiencies. Phone: 305-294-5723.

Sugarloaf Key KOA, Rt 2, Box 680, P.O. Box 469, Summerland Key FL 33042. Phone: 305-745-3549. This 14-acre park is on the water, oceanside at MM 20. Pool, hot tub, sandy beach, store, marina, boats, canoes. Restaurant.

INDEX

ADDITIONAL READING

Other Adventure Travel Books and Tour Guides from Hunter Publishing:

BEST DIVES OF THE WESTERN HEMISPHERE

by Jon Huber, Joyce Huber & Christopher Lofting

Over 200 sites for the best diving in Latin America, the Caribbean, California & Hawaii. Maps & color photos throughout. Everything you need to know to plan your dive trip. "Essential for the serious or beginning diver." Dr. Susan Cropper, DVM. *5 3/8 x 8 pbk/320 pp/$17.95*

THE ADVENTURE GUIDE TO PUERTO RICO*

by Harry S. Pariser

The best all-around guide to the island. History, people & culture, plus what to see, where to stay, where to dine. All color, with maps.
5 3/8 x 8 pbk/224 pp/$15.95

JAMAICA: A VISITOR'S GUIDE*

by Harry S. Pariser

All-around guide for travellers -- what to see and do, where to stay, how to get around. All color, with maps. *5 3/8 x 8/256 pp/$15.95*

THE ADVENTURE GUIDE TO JAMAICA*

by Steve Cohen

A classic, now completely updated, this is the definitive guide to outdoor activities in Jamaica—from hiking to white-water rafting, from scuba to horse-trekking. All color, with maps. *5 3/8 x 8/288 pp/$15.95*

THE ADVENTURE GUIDE TO COSTA RICA*

by Harry S. Pariser

The most detailed guide. Exhaustive coverage of the history, culture, unique wildlife, what to see. All color. *5 3/8 x 8 pbk/360 pp/$16.95*

THE ADVENTURE GUIDE TO BELIZE

by Harry S. Pariser

With some of the best diving in the world, 1000-ft waterfalls, virgin rainforest, 500 species of birds, Belize is a naturalist's paradise. The latest & best color guide. *5 3/8 x 8 pbk/256 pp/$15.95*

These books can be found at the best bookstores or you can order directly. Send your check (add $2.50 to cover postage & handling) to:

HUNTER PUBLISHING, INC.
300 RARITAN CENTER PKWY
EDISON NJ 08818

Write or call (908) 225-1900 for our free color catalog describing these and many other travel guides and maps to every destination on earth.

Titles marked with an asterisk can be obtained in the UK through Moorland Publishing.